Table of Contents

Introduction ....
    Donel Poston

Forward. ....
    Alex Taylor

Chapter 1: Degree Seeking Student
    Donel Poston 1

Chapter 2: Brave Enough to Change
    Brett Richardson 15

Chapter 3: Even in the Deepest of Depths
    Steve Jennings 23

Chapter 4: Turning Obstacles into Opportunities
    Jose Duarte 41

Chapter 5: Tore From the Flag by Men of the Cloth
    James Wilson 53

Chapter 6: My Two Roads Travelled
    Adrian Woodard 71

Chapter 7: The Exponentially of 1° Degree
    Brian Fiore 79

Epilogue
    Rabbi Brian Zachary Mayer 95

Introduction

"A small body of determined spirits fired by an unquenchable faith in their mission can alter the course of history."

-Mahatma Ghandi

Introduction

I take pleasure in participating in this project with such admirable gentlemen. This project speaks volumes to where we've been, but most importantly where we're going and how we arrived there. This project is based on the concept of how we obtained freedom by degrees or levels in our life. Moreso, the different perspectives, ethnicities, backgrounds, and affiliations that shaped our views in the past and the evolution of those views, which ultimately allowed us to elevate, setting ourselves free from stagnation and distorted thinking.

In addition, this is a kaleidoscope of personalities, attitudes, and visions. These gentlemen are teachers and mentors revered by students and staff. They have reached a place in their lives where the discovery of purpose is on the precipice, and freedom is on the horizon. This is a genuine attempt at rummaging through our past and recognizing how each mistake, experience, and revelation was a stepping block towards freedom. This may not be how we envisoned life as children, but what we realized as men.

As a result of warped thinking, all of us have received lengthy sentences, and for that reason, there is an unlimited amount of jewels to be taken from each individual an applied to life. There is hope in each story, maybe enough to change some lives for the better. I realize between us all we have caused enough hurt to last a lifetime. However, what lies on the other end of that stick is resilience, accountability, and wisdom — a resource currently unavailable to the youth because mass incarceration has caused a drought on men like these. The streets have become an arid region; the children malnourished because they lack the presence of leadership, which is vital to their growth.

Mind you, leading may have not brought us to our current residence, but its definitely going to get us back home. For that matter, I humbly ask you to embark on the journey of reading Freedom by Degrees. Thank you.

Donel Poston

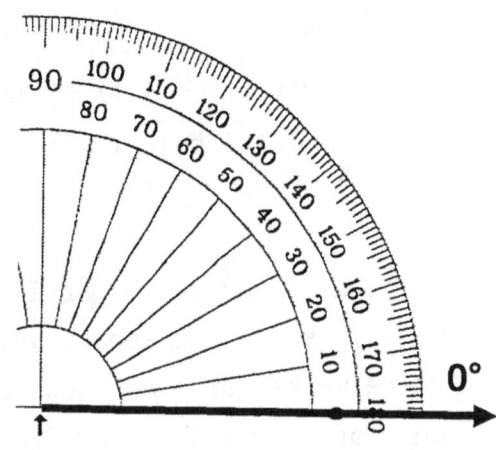

START SOMEWHERE

FORWARD

In 2017, my dear friend and rabbi, Brian Mayer, asked members of his congregation to write to his incarcerated pen pal, James Wilson. Exactly five years ago to the day, I sat down at my desk and penned a note to a complete stranger.

At the time, I didn't know my letter would hold any significance. I wrote it, simply because I was asked. I didn't realize it would lay the foundation for a continuing and valued friendship, which has spanned hundreds of cards and letters over the years. As I've come to know James, he has shown me his valuable efforts to create rehabilitative self-help programs, and to mentor his fellow inmates at High Desert State Prison.

As a newly-married, white, middle-class, female, computer programmer and writer, I had the privilege of growing up in a safe community, where a good education and a college degree were the norm, not the exception. Until I met James, I had few meaningful or long-lasting relationships with those who didn't have a similar background.

My correspondence with James has not only created a deep and meaningful friendship; it has also opened my eyes to a world I did not know existed. I now have a keen awareness to the plight of inmates and the scant rehabilitative resources provided to them. I have realized how so many young people are categorically denied a shot at the American Dream before they have a chance to start their lives.

I hope, after reading this book, that you will share my awareness, and that you'll join the chorus of voices that support criminal justice reform and programs for at-risk youth. The majority of prisoners will eventually be released, and we desperately need programs that rehabilitate, rather than punish, our country's inmates.

The stories in *Freedom by Degrees* are raw and disturbing. They describe how poverty, gangs, a lack of education, and trauma, interrupt young lives and put them on the wrong path. These biographies describe how James and his mentees struggle every day to move beyond their troubling pasts, and to educate and rehabilitate themselves. It is these tremendous efforts that make me proud to know my friend James and his fellow inmates at High Desert State Prison.

Alex Taylor
15 February 2022

DONEL POSTON

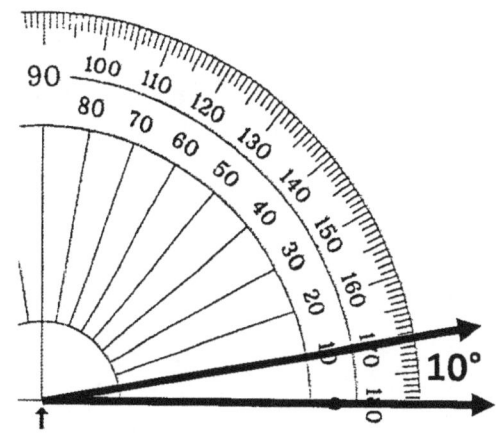

7

DEVELOP A VISION

"To share your weakness is to make yourself vulnerable;
to make yourself vulnerable is to show your strength"

Degree Seeking Student
-Criss Jami

There was a time when I didn't give a fuck. I had lost control of what I stood for. I wasn't an angry kid, but I can remenber when the pain began. I think the emotion was born when we moved to the 20s, and my parents had got into this heated fight that ended with gunfire, and eventually my dad and I moving to Alabama.

However, before that, we lived in another part of east Oakland, 73rd and Fresno, where I spent the bulk of my childhood. I was a happy kid, a contrast to my environment. 1981 was the introduction of the crack epidemic in my life, and where I lived seem like the crack capital.

Oakland is not known for any symbolic gangs such as Bloods and Crips or Vicelords and Disciples. Oakland operates on a different system, turfs. In the '80s, there were only a few main turfs that dominated the Oakland streets. Where I lived at it was dominated by the 69th Village, aka the Mob.

The Mob was orchestrated by Felix Mitchell, but it was Lil' D—Darryl Reed— who would become infamous amongst those in my era. If where I lived was the crack capital, Lil' D was definitely the president. One house over was the housing authority apartments, right across the streets were more, the Mob controlled them both. Ever present were young men wearing L.D.I t-shirts - Lil' Darryl Incorporated. Whether he had any formal knowledge about business structure I don't know, because clearly he was running an oligopoly. There were only a few main people running crack operations back in them days, he was a staple and a barrier to entry.

This was my life, this is where I gained my insight into the street life. There were three elementary schools that were in close proximity to the village and my house: Lockwood, Webster, and Markham. If you attended any of those schools between '82 and '88, somebody in your family was directly or indirectly associated with the Mob. For me, it was my brothers and the neighborhood. All the kids I played with, went to school with, or met in the streets had some connection to the Mob. All my brother's friends had something to do with the Mob. In '82, halfway through the year, I turned six. What the hell was I doing having any knowledge about a notorious criminal faction like the Mob? What's crazy, if I hadn't possessed any knowledge about the Mob it would've been especially hard to navigate through the streets of Oakland.

On the other hand, what was also present were residual effects of what the

Black Panthers had established. Scrolled on various walls, up and down the MacArthur strip, were derogatory epithets created by what the Panthers were trying to form: unity, rebellion, and namely a call for justice against the government and the Oakland Police. I relate this account to some graffiti that read "Fuck the Pigs". At six years old, I couldn't figure out for the life of me why anyone wanted to fuck pigs. Consequently, those words are forever etched in my memory.

The Uhuru House, where I first began to understand some of the Panther rhetoric, was a beacon for Black kids in the '70s and the '80s. The free meals, the literature, that community was my introduction to Black power. The Uhuru house was located on Ritchie and MacArthur. Occassionally, in the summer, my friends and I would stray from the neighborhood and find ourselves getting free lunches that they provided for low income kids. I don't remember what was in the lunches, but I do remember the Panther's newspaper. Notably, a black panther on top of a news article was most fascinating, especially to a child. I fashion myself a great reader; by that time I had won a reading award, so I read every inch of that paper, even if I didn't understand half of what I was reading.

I spent a lot of time with my two older brothers because my parents had a steady income at their respected jobs. My mom worked at the Oakland Army Base, my dad worked for Alameda County Transit. My brothers and I had different dads, like most families that you encounter in the ghetto. That didn't make us no less brothers. I was a latchkey kid from the first to the sixth grade. When I wasn't at home by myself, Mikey and Robbie were tasked the responsibility of looking over me. Like most teenagers, little brothers slowed them down. Not for my middle brother, Robbie, he'd drag me along and do whatever it was that he was doing. That is, drinking, smoking, fighting, shooting, it didn't matter, as long as I was safe he'd continue doing whatever it was that he was doing.

Consequently, getting high was a mainstay in my house. If it wasn't the shoebox lid or the green box tucked under the couch, it was the triple beam scale on my parents dresser. These small details left an indelible mark on my conscious. My memory is filled with weed runs with my mother, my brothers getting high on the back porch while my parents were at work, and my mama crouched behind the stove smoking crack.

The neighborhood kids had been joking that my mom was a basehitter. It seem innocent enough, but crack cocaine was described as a base rock. If you smoked crack, you used a basepipe. So, if you took a basehit, that meant you used a basepipe to smoke crack. Long story short, my mama smoked crack! How could I believe that?

I was an innocent child searching for his mother when I entered the kitchen. What I saw paralyze me, but from that day on I wasn't as naive. I began to recognize the subtle moves my parents were making, such as sending my brothers to go cop dope for them. The times my dad would carry me along with him to his friend's house and they'd be in the opposing room getting high.

The cat was out the bag. The whole house was using some form of cocaine except for me. My brothers began smoking grimmies — cracked laced joints — in the seventh grade. My mom and dad altered between crack and coke. In the '80s, coke was seen as a rich man's high, crack was a cheaper more lethal form. In retrospect, that triple beam scale was utilized for something. I know it was cocaine because I tasted it.

One morning I went to get some socks out of the dresser drawer I shared with my parents. Tucked behind the Old Spice cologne, slightly peeking from behind the mirror, was this machine that resembled an erector set. It was new to me. I was curious. What led me to swipe my finger acoss the metal plate is a mystery. All I know is my whole mouth went numb like I was at the dentist.

My curiosity didn't stop there. I had watched my parents and my brothers roll enough joints that by the third grade I was stealing Zig-Zags and scraping the seeds, stems, and shake from the shoebox lid, folding it in some paper, and going to share that with my friends across the street. I did that a few times.

At such a young age I was exposed to so much criminal activity. I seen the guns being sold. I watched the fraud transpire. The drug transactions. The lying and stealing. This was the foundation to my youth, my core beliefs. The people I most looked up to made me familiar to the things that I should have looked down on. They shape my perception, flaunting opportunities that should've never been made available.

In addition to all the chaos, I was a good student. That is, I was very aware. I loved to read, and could string thoughts together and make deductions about my surroundings. This worked well for me in school and in the streets. But because I was so young, mostly school. However, any opportunity that presented itself I was applying it to the streets.

I believe my first semblance of hustling came with me pumping gas. Where I lived was just a few blocks from the Eastmont mall. Back then, there stood a gas station on the corner of the mall parking lot, and another located directly across the street. My friends and I would show up to the gas station around 4 pm, sometime after school, riding our bikes. We'd leave the bikes by the water and the air pump. At that time, most of my friends did not know how to articulate themselves well. My competitive advantage was my delivery and my innocent appearance. "Excuse me ma'am/sir, can I pump your gas please", oppose to, "A, can I pump yo gas". It worked like a charm. However, somedays it wouldn't be that easy, especially when I arrived with the kids from the Ville.

These kids were cut from a different cloth. They did it out of necessity, I did it for the thrill. They embodied an element of savagery that I didn't possess at that time. Aggressive is an understatement, fervant is more like it.

Those days were marked by running from pump to pump, fighting for position, just to ask could I pump someones gas. That's when my brain outwitted their brawn. They'd scamper over to the pump, I'd just sit back an wait, use a little finesse and land me a few customers. Most times, I would end up on the short end of the stick, that's if we're talking monetary; but what I gained in militance was priceless.

I got myself involved in stealing early on. It was short-lived, but as I got older it became a hustle. As a child I stole candy and sold it at school, but for some reason I had an aversion for stealing and I quit. Unsurprisingly, when I got to high school, thievery resurrectd itself. I made it a staple in my activities. We stole Polo from Macy's, shoes and boots fom Nordstrom's and Nautica. From then on, the hustle got real.

It began as a way to gain status and fit-in. Besides, if you had the freshest clothes or money to squander on weed you were cool. We'd take trips to the Oakland hills and steal from the unguarded supermarkets. Seemingly, we discovered that the liquor stores in the ghetto, owned by our Yemeni friends, would purchase the alcohol in bulk. For that reason, we'd set out across the greater Bay Area stealing from grocery stores, liquor outlets, and drug stores (Walgreens, Rite-Aid, and CVS).

Stealing was a gateway. Next thing you know, I'm selling drugs, doing fraud, and carrying guns and committing robberies.

In hindsight, I see that the root of my rebellion rested with what I saw my mother doing in the kitchen in the '80s.

Prior to things getting out of hand, I was an aspiring student. There was a period in my life when I felt like I could emerge from this tumult victorious. I was a member of the GATE program in junior high school, attending Cal Berkeley for summer school. I attended Saturday college at a local community college while in high school. I attended dinner dances and proms, things seemed promising.

Meanwhile, at home, my mom was still battling addiction. I was sad. I felt abandoned. No mater what I did, she failed to recognize my efforts. I'd bring home 4.0s, I was on the honor roll, I wrote magnificent papers, all I wanted was someone to validate my accomplishments. She spent more time in the bathroom then she did attending to her responsibilities. Her addiction got so bad that she began stealing from me.

My dad and I moved to Alabama in the summer of '88. Following a triumphant drug run, my father needed to get back to his country roots. It took us two days on Greyhound. After about a year my dad regained his sobriety. After two years, I couldn't take it much longer, I moved back.

However, when I moved back, my dad use to send me money. I used it for school, school clothes, and small outings with my friends. At first, I would store my money in the drawer in my bathroom (at this time I had my own bathroom), until it began to disappear. I blamed it on being irresponsible at first. Then I accused my friends. Neither was the case.

Surprisingly, I woke one night when my mom was rummaging through my pockets. What I seen was someone that looked like my mama. She had hazel eyes like my mama. Her skin was brown like my mamas. But the person who came in my room wasn't my mama, that was a monster.

I was hurt. I felt betrayed. And most of all, I was shocked that it had come to this. In the end, I would turn the money loose, and cry myself to sleep. I believed once I returned from Alabama things would change. Well, they did. She got better concealing it from everyone else. Although she had moved from that toxic environment, those demons still followed her. I was still experiencing neglect, suffering mostly from the lack of emotional support and attention. My step-father didn't use drugs or drink, but some how he put up with my mother's shit.

For that reason, from the time I encountered that monster, I spiraled out of control. Weed had been a distant memory before I left for Alabama, which was in the sixth grade. Now, heading for the 10th grade, I was more conscious than ever. I gave in. I was smoking weed regularly. I began drinking, hanging in the wrong crowds, stealing. My grades began to drop. The rest of my high school years were a blur.

In spite of that, at 16 I left home. After a botched robbery attempt, where I was a passenger in a vehicle that ran into a house, I was almost sent to juvenile hall. When the police arrived I was in possession of a gun. The juvenile courts gave me an ultimatum, go to jail or return to Alabama with my dad. In route to Alabama, I had a layover in Arizona. From there, I convinced the ticket agent to refund me my money and send me back to California. I never made it to Alabama, nor did I make it back to my mom's house either.

As luck would have it, my friends had just received a huge record deal with Jive records. A year prior, they had graduated from our high school. My boy had his own apartment. That's where I would stay for the time being.

Strangely enough, everything that I thought I wanted were the things that I didn't need. I wanted freedom. I wanted to stay high. I wanted control. I wanted away from my mother. I wanted to live the rap life. Unfortunately, all this was a recipe for disaster.

Life was moving fast. I was in and out of the state, tagging along with my friends while they performed shows. I was still underage, but I indulged in drugs and alcohol like a rockstar. Even when there wasn't a show, my days consisted of getting high, making music, and hanging out.

That persisted for several more years, which meant that I fell deeper and deeper into addiction. Funny though, I didn't realize I was creating a toxic lifestyle. I woke up getting high. I got high out of boredom. I got high when I was excited. I got high before I went to sleep. Some nights we didn't go to sleep, we'd stay up getting high entertaining friends. After all, this is everything that I thought I wanted.

In fact, after I moved on I hit rock bottom. I was couch surfing. I lived in the backseat of a car. I was now stealing food just so that I could eat.

Shortly thereafter, my crime wave began. In order to support my habits, I began selling crack and weed. Ironically, I ended up hustling a couple of blocks from the Ville. Then I moved to fraud, then back to selling drugs. I managed to get away with a few robberies, until I was eventually caught.

As a result, I was sent to the county jail. First for selling weed. Then, I tried to rob a bike shop. My friend and I escaped, but soon after got caught and sent to the county jail. This was the beginning of a very long rapsheet.

As a matter of fact, for the next 25 years I would spend the majority of my life in and out of prison. I have had three prison numbers, done seven terms, a string of violations, and now, on my third number, I have received a sentence of 72 years to life. I was charged with second degree murder and attempted murder.

Throughout my prison journey, then and now, I have attempted to make slight changes in my life. For instance, while doing time for the bike shop robbery, I earned my GED. At that time, I was only a year or two removed from high school, plus I had an affinity for learning (I took and received my GED in 30 days). My first prison term, I encountered some elder incarcerated men that took notice to my voracious reading habits. They begin supplying me with books of substance; books that lead me to understand what the Uhuru house was really about it, people who had stood up for the movement.

Although I would return to prison a many times after that, those subtle advances were the beginning steps to my degrees of freedom. As I matured, I began to search for knowledge, looking for my purpose, searching for where I fit in in the science of life. During that prison term, I was introduced to Islam. I took my Shahada - declaration of faith - after reading the Quran and interacting with some other younger Muslims. Although I wanted so badly to adhere to the tenets of the religion, I was not yet ready to honor my contract with God. My youthful disposition would prevent me from rising to my next level of freedom.

The last term that I did before embarking on a life sentence, I was housed at a CCF (Community Correctional Facility) in Shafter, CA. Upon release, I moved to Las Vegas for a short stint. I returned to Oakland because parole was barking down my throat. Consequently, I landed a job at a work release program, Golden State Works-Cal Trans. After nearly 20 years, in and out of the system, I finally began to feel a sense of normalcy.

Monday through Friday, I'd awake at 4:30 am, shower, dress, and head for the busstop. For the first time I had created a routine. I began to understand what civil people do, in an attempt at making a honest living. Until one night, I was visited by an intruder at my house.

It had been a long day of filmming. Alongside my job at Cal Trans, I was an amateur videographer and photographer, skills acquired when I attended Ex'pressions Digital Art College. Lying in my bed, in a marijauna induced coma, an armed intruder burst through my bedroom window. After a few minutes of trying to unarm the gunmen, I was shot several times in the chest, which almost ended my life. A bullet entered near my heart, punctured my lunges, knocked out my spleen, and lodged in my back. I spent nearly a month in the hospital, fighting off infection and trying to regain my health.

My sense of normalcy was destroyed. I believed when I was shot that I needed to defend myself. I was paranoid, scared, and confused. For that reason, I armed myself, a decision I would regret. Now my daughters would be without a father.

As a result of a few failed relationships, I help create five beautiful little ladies. Nakalia, Alana, Yazmeen, Aniya, and Dawn are my pride and joy. With Nakalia being my oldest and Dawn the youngest, I would try my best to see that my girls had what they wanted. Sometimes I'd break the law just to provide. What I realize though, is that material presents can never take the place of presence, a fact neglected when I chose to acquire a firearm.

Although I'm on good terms with my children's mothers, I can't help but to think of the resentment they must harbor for me in my absence. Each time I was whisked away on a violation or a new term, I was also missing out on my opportunity to be an active parent. What I would soon find out is that no amount of letters, phone calls, or prison art would make up for the time away from my daughters.

I was so enslaved by drugs and the street life that I lost sight of my priorities, my daughters. The frequent trips to prison would further the distance of a relationship that was already spotty. My selfish ways wouldn't allow me to part with our most valuable resource, time. I was forever trying to bust-a-move, make something happen, or come up. Never being able to sit down long enough to give my daughters that much needed undivided attention. Soon I would learn.

My mom and I always had a running joke about my frequent prison visits. She would always tell my aunts, friends, or kids that I was off at college. Well, on March 21, 2014 I had been sentenced to serve 72 years-to-life in the California Department of Corrections. I was about to enter the hidden university. All those violations and new terms were nothing but mere semesters compared to this sentence. This time I would be a degree seeking student. The only problem is, the date of the graduation would depend on my day of reckoning.

> There are three things you need to get over any big hurt:
> Understanding, Forgiveness, and Closure.

The hardest thing to swallow was the time that they handed me. Not because I didn't think that I could handle it, but what I was about to put my love ones through. Its selfish to think that just because you're locked in the cell or stuck behind the wall that you're doing time by youself. It pains me to hear my mother talk about her bad days. I hurt when I hear my daughters talk about milestones that they've reached and I couldn't be there to support them.

Moreso, when my chidren's mothers are overwhelmed with financial burdens, and I'm not present to provide assistance.

Immediately upon arriving at High Desert State Prison, I had to learn about accountability. Accountability is like math, in order to retain it you must practice it repetitiously. What I fail to realize is that nobody sent me to prison but myself. Oftentimes, you hear people talking about why everything and everyone but themselves are the reason for why their in prison. We make excuses for our choices and blame our circumstances on the outcome. It was time to start looking at my decisions, and how they were affecting everything and everyone around me. Whats plausible is that it all begins with you. Once you come into age and your moral compass is set, the direction you take hinges on your decisions; choices are many, decisions are final. I am here because of the decisions I made. I had plenty of choices, I chose the wrong one. Not just in my case, but in life as well.

Being that I had spent so much time in prison as a young adult, when I was sentenced I knew everything that I wasn't gonna do. I wouldn't be wasting my time telling stories, talking about the what ifs and I could haves. I definitely didn't see myself chasing cigarettes and sticks — joints. No more honey bears full of white lightning — distilled alcohol — or folgers jars full of pruno. All that time I wasted. Everything that I did and did not do before was part of the reason why I was here now.

For that reason, I was adamant about creating a strategic plan and sticking to it. That involved setting short-term goals and having a long-term landscape. I planned on writing several books. I needed to get a degree. And I needed to do some deep introspection through self-help.

In business there are some barriers that are hard to overcome. Since I was planning on handling my business, I needed to think about what would be stopping me from reaching my goals. Just like in business, social and the political environment are barriers that may be out of your control. Well, in prison, social and the political environment play a big part of you succeeding. There's not much you can do about who you socialize with and the political environment on a level IV yard. The politics are divisive. People die over tables and workout areas. The environment, at least where I was at, made it hard for you to succeed.

There wasn't any access to self-help groups (the signs in the dayroom were dated 24 months prior to me signing up). The college coordinator told me that

I'd never get into college because I was so far down the waiting list. And getting a job in any capacity was next to nil because the occupants were longtime offenders who couldn't get their points down to leave, so they hardly ever transferred.

For that matter, I created a routine that was conducive to my strategic plan. I woke up early to make prayer. Thereafter, I would do about 500 pushups, eat, and begin studying. My studies consisted of reading, reading up on my case, and writing my attorney, as well as meeting my quota on the number of pages to complete my book. I'd do that til' 11 am, resume my workout, birdbath, then eat. I'd end my days by typing letters to family, friends, and resource centers. After playing a little Jeopardy with my celly, I was off to sleep.

This routine set precedence for my short-term goals. I like to think that I made hardship into habit. In looking for results, there must be some consistency. That's what my daily activites required. I mentioned before that repetition is a way to implement change, creating a routine is an elaborate process that you do consistently. Once I began this routine, I wanted to do it until I felt funny not doing it.

Consequently, the political environment demanded too much of me. I wasn't willing to forego my time for someone elses agenda. I didn't see me taking anymore unwanted risk due to some outdated politics. For that reason, I chose to step away from the mainline. Besides, I was up for transfer, but really I wanted to make sure that I had a clear path to the goals that I was setting. The change of environment was a much needed step in order for me to fully embrace what I was trying to accomplish. However, I battled with my ego, fought with my pride, and ultimately, I prayed on it; God had me.

In addition to accountability, my willingness to let go of that environment showed me that I was ready to continue seeking my degrees of freedom.

As a matter of fact, things started to come together fast. Once I made that move, I became a facilitator in AVP (Alternative to Violence Program). I was chosen to participate in a college pilot program that only permitted 50 students to enter. I finished my first manuscript. Things didn't stop there, I continued by accepting the position as the Amir (religious leader) in our local muslim community.

What I had been longing to do years before finally was available for me to explore. I made a vow to God and myself not to miss another prayer. I increased my knowledge on the history and the formalities of the Islamic culture.

Although I had been active in the Islamic community on the mainline, I was able to see the many facets of Islam once I was in my new environment.

Seemingly, what I had began to develop was a foundation. I like to call it the trifecta. That is, if I could maintain a steady increase and balance of my mind, body, and soul I could potentially make at least a one percent daily change that would eventually change my perspective on how I viewed life in the past.

Along the way, I managed to help those around me. Not only did I participate in these self-help groups, I facilitated them; I created them; and most importantly, I live them. My daily actions prove to be a model for what I stood for. When I spoke to people they didn't have a problem listening. Because I made myself vulnerable, it allowed others to be vulnerable, which meant that we could grow together. I spent several years in the Juvenile Diversion Program, which help me inventory my past. I could now pass the information that I learned about myself to others in similar situations.

I could feel myself evolving. The process was cathartic. The trifecta was healthy for my well-being. I continued to build on what I had began to establish. For each group I attended, I was able to pluck a jewel from it. Afterwhile, I had a trove of information at my disposal.

The results were amazing. After three years, I had received three Associate degrees, I had published three Urban Street Novels, I had completed nearly 30 self-help groups, obtain a certificate of completion in entrepreneurship, completed a mentorship in the Juvenile Diversion Program, and a list of other accomplishments. I was becoming the person that I set out to be.

In addition, I was approached about being in another ground breaking pilot program. The idea behind the program was that fellow incarcerated men could potentially do a better job assisting other incarcerated men succeed in getting their GED, high school diploma, or college degree. Studies showed that men with adverse childhood experiences, learning disabilities, or who have been absent from the academic environment put up barriers to learning. So, who best to convey the message? Other men who have travelled down those same dark roads.

Mind you, this wasn't an easy task. The training lasted nearly two years. The first year, Mr. Giles, who happens to be an exceptional selfless human being, took us through the rigors of understanding learning theories by Bloom, Mezirow, Maslow, and many more. We held meetings daily, discussed effective ways on how to assist Adult Basic Education and voluntary students in our community. We did presentations, wrote essays, and learned about learning and teaching. We built the program from the ground up. The structure, the design, and the daily duties. Then finally, the Department of Corrections and Education picked up the program, which meant another 700 hours of training and test composed by the state. It felt like an uphill battle. Not to mention, the constant pushback from staff who thought that education was a sham, and all we were doing was wiggling in and out of buildings.

However, once the training was complete, the GED scores went through the roof. The college program was provided some much needed assistance. We developed RAC (Rehabilitative Achievement Credits) classes that allowed students assistance with earning their GED, as well as a way to earn time off of their sentence. We provided assistance for nonenglish-speaking students. Our goal was to get the whole yard a GED.

Meanwhile, while training to become a Peer Literacy Mentor/Tutor, I created several self-help groups with the assistance of a few other men on the yard. We created Life Choices after the Juvenile Diversion Program disbanded. This program allowed the participants to do some introspection. Starting with your earliest memory, tracking those good and bad events that affected your life. We created Reaching Out From Within. This program helped participants reach inside themselves and face their struggles. We created New H.E.A.R.T.S (Helping Everybody Articulate Rehabilitation Through Storytelling). This group provided a space for men to talk about their problems, in an open forum, with others on a similar topic. In our final project, "Write Our Wrongs", a concept inspired by Shaka Senghor, is a composition of Letter to our victims, poems, and short stories. We published the book, made it available on Amazon, donating all the money to victims and to support charities.

Success doesn't come easy. The only way that I would be successful in reaching the level of freedom I was searching for is to continue to make positive strides at changing the way I thought in the past. In order to do that, I continue to educate and rehabilitate myself. I need to continue to fortify the relationships that I'm building with my children. No more being selfish, only selfless.

Furthermore, I'm just one semester away from earning my Bachelor degree. I intend on going for my MBA. But still and all, no matter how many groups I finish, no matter how many degrees I get, I'll always continue to elevate until I reach my freedom by degrees.

Donel Poston
AT-2512

BRET RICHARDSON

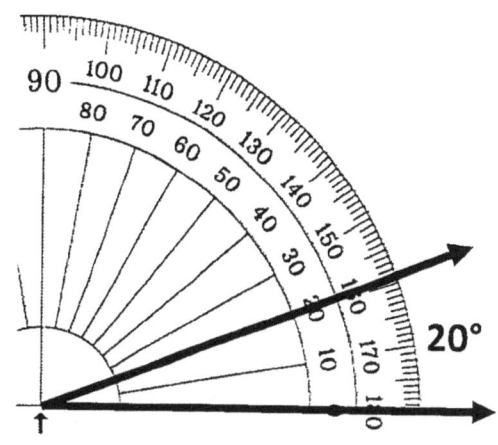

CHALLENGE YOURSELF

Brave Enough to Change

One of the most daunting challenges I've ever had to face in life was that of self-analysis. It took me almost 40 years to gather the courage to "step outside of myself", so to speak, identify my many character flaws, and acknowledge that I'd been mentally, emotionally, and spiritually incarcerated virtually my entire life. Most men, especially those whom share similar backgrounds and experiences as I, have been conditioned, in some form or another, to believe that any emotional expression, other than some form of masculine agression, is considered weak, or unmanly.

Me, nor any other man that I've ever known, has never been ready or willing to openly admit that they experienced insecurities, self-doubt, shame, embarrassment, or any other emotion that may have had them labeled a "sucka". I, like many other men being raised in my environment, was taught to "suck it up", to remain "chin-up and chest-out", and above all else, not to be a "sucka". You see, in the inner-city streets of America, that word "sucka" weighs a megaton, and ranks just beneath a snitch or rapist. Suckas weren't down, suckas got beat-up, robbed, or worst, killed. So, as a young boy, it was thoroughly ingrained in my young impressionable mind that I was not to be a sucka.

I was about seven or eight years old when my beloved uncle was murdered. I remember clear as day the way my mother screamed when the news was brought to our doorstep. I remember my uncle laying face down on a dirty matress, the back of his head bloody from the single gunshot wound. Also, I vividly remember that a month later my grandfather being murdered. He was stabbed and shot several times before being hung and then disgarded in a dumpster as if he wasn't even human. As I watched them pull my grandfather's lifeless corpse from the trash dumpster I think that's when I subconsciously, at eight years old, made the decision to not only be labeled a sucka, but also to never be somebody's victim.

Needless to say, being exposed to that level of violence at such an early age, or any age for that matter, truly traumatized me. Although I didn't fully realize how much so until way later in life. The confusion, hurt, and anger I felt toward a father who refused to even acknowledge my existence, only added fuel to the fire that burned away my innocence. By age 13 I was running the streets with men old enough to have been my father; smoking weed, drinking alcohol, selling drugs, and disobeying all ten commandments.

The heroin and crack epidemic created celebrities, superstars, and living legends of my older relatives and friends, which inflamed my infatuation and lust for the fast street-life and the criminal activities that accompanied it.

Subsequently, the emergence and explosion of gangster rap music and cult-classic films such as New Jack City, Boyz-N-The-Hood, Menace II Society, and Belly romanticized and glorified the criminalistic lifestyle that many of us had been living in real life. Ultimately, desensitizing a whole generation, I included, to the value of human life, drug usage, violence, and the impact our decisions have on the communities we inhabit.

By my 21st birthday. I'd done time in juvenile hall, youth authority, county jail, and the state prison. Also, I'd lost more family and friends than I could count to gun violence and drug abuse. At this point in my young life I was completely immersed in the streets, a personification of the criminal lifestyle.

In a subconscious attempt to "fit in" and simultaneously protect myself from all the heartache, heart break, pain, and frustration of my life experiences. And simply being born black in a country that, semmigly, automatically viewed me as a threat, I'd cultivated the persona of a man with nothing to lose and everything to gain by not giving a fuck about anything or anybody outside of my inner-circle. And though this was a form of tribalism, I now understand that I had become imprisoned by my own criminal ideology, false pride, and misplaced honor. My moral compass was in dire need of recalibration.

Prison only managed to enhance my distorted perception of life, and corrupted codes of conduct. The prison system is like a world within a world, with much different rules and regulations from the societal norm. On top of the official rules that must be adhered to to avoid write-ups, there are even more frustrating, confusing, often petty, and rigidly enforced "prisoner rules" that must be adhered to to avoid "beat-downs"!

Just imagine being unwillingly cast in a season-long episode of Big Brother, Game of Thrones, and Survivor all rolled-up into one show. You are surrounded by a bunch of hardened criminals, some you know and most you wish that you never met on this side of life!

The whole transition from freedom to incarceration, with all its prison politics, is enough to drive any normal person completely insane. So I guess one would have to be abnormally insane to some degree to survive this place for any extended period of time? Ironically, I began to find my inner freedom through my physical imprisonment.

At age 30, as I sat in my county jail cell, all alone, charged with possession of an assault weapon, armed robbery, and first degree murder, my feelings weren't of sadness, anger, or fear, but more so of utter relief. I had become mentally, emotionally, and spiritually fatigued of the destructive lifestyle I'd led for so very long. At that time I felt 40 years older than I actually was. Sitting in my cell, I got down on my hands and knees sincerly thanking God for placing me in jail.

My life had become a constant uncontrollable chaos. Outside of my children and family, no one's life mattered to me. Where my heart had once beat, filled with love for life, was now just an empty chasm. I had allowed myself to become cold and callous. My attitude toward extreme acts of violence was nonchalant at best. I wasn't so naive to have wondered how I ended up living in such darkness. I knew just how I had turned down a path of moral destitution: I had made the choice earlier on in life. The lifestyle I had chosen to live was celebrated and encouraged in just about everything around me. The music I listen to, the movies I watched, family who looked up to me for protection and financial security, friends and the females I dated who praised me for being a beast in the streets. Hell, even watching how our government annihilated whomever it perceived as a threat on national television. All this lended to my mindstate of: Respect my mind, fear my wrath, or lord have mercy on you!

So, there I sat in that cell, facing the possibility of life in prison, regretting the choices and decisions I'd made in life. Not regretting those decisions because I'd been caught, but because of what and who I'd become.

I remember about a few days before I was arrested, I had asked my mother and the mother of my children to pray with me. When they asked why, I told them that I could feel either my death approaching or a prison cell, which really isn't that much of a difference! I now realize that it was my very soul that was exhausted with all the bullshit that had become my life. A man can only endure, experience, and partake in so much debauchery before he either comes to his senses, or succumb to his inevitable self-destruction.

I was in my third year of incarceration when I took the first baby-step in my very long journey to inner freedom. One day I was at a visit with the mother of my children, and I was talking about how sick I was of jail, and how ready I was to come home. I don't know why but, she suddenly looked at me and told me that I wasn't ready.

Now of course my first thought was WTF! But I understood what she was saying.

She knew that if I was released back into society at that time in my life, still with a heart and mind full of anger, vengence, selfishness, and unforgiveness I would set the world on fire; and damned who got burned. In my heart of hearts I knew that I was not ready, least of all deserving of being set free just to torment my community.

I had once heard, in order to rise from its own ashes, a phoenix must first burn. This is when the first soul-cleansing flames of adversity begin to burn away all the demented and delusional principles I'd lived by my entire life. It was as if my perception of the way I thought about life in general had changed over night.

Maybe it was maturity finally hitting me. The traumatic experience of facing life in prison, God waking my game up, or the impact of all three. Whatever the case, I just know I was in my cell listening to these cats a few cells down from mine bragging about their crimes, and what they were going to do when they got out. As I'm laying on my bunk all I could think about was how incredibly stupid everything coming out of their mouths sounded. At first I thought I was getting old, but I noticed that I continually begin to dispute my old way of thinking.

It is said that, God transforms people once we seek change in the way we think. I read in Ephesians 4:22-23, "[To] throw off your old evil nature and your former way of life, which is rotten through and through, full of lust and deception. Instead, there must be a spiritual renewal of your thoughts and attitudes". To me, that made sense in the world. How could I ever hope to change my behavior if I never changed the way I was thinking?

From that day forward, I made the decision to actively change my thought process. Once I had identified my desperate need for a change in thinking, I no longer wished to be imprisoned by the criminal mentality and ideologies I'd held for so long. Like I said in the beginning, it was more than a challenge to confront my inner-demons and character flaws but, once I admitted to myself that I was selfish, self-centered, unempathetic, narcissistic, and insecure, it was actually a relief to unload all the emotional baggage.

I was finally breaking free of my old way of thinking. I had begun the process of self-analysis; assessing my relationship with family and friends, and how I communicated with people I came in contact with. By gradually changing the way I thought, I not only changed my behavior and principles, I also changed the way I treated people. I began to be a lot less judgmental and

more empathetic toward others outside my immediate family. I began to take full responsibility for my actions and make more conscious decisions to better live in peace with everyone around me. For so long I thought, and truly believed, if I went harder, had more money, drove a better car, wore the best clothes, had sex with the most prettiest and well-endowed women, that I would be more accepted and respected by my peers.

In hindsight, accomplishing any and all of those won me no long-term fulfillment or accolades. What I did accomplish with my old ways of thinking and beliefs were a life-sentence, the taking of human lives, making enemies of my victim's family members, depriving my children of their father's love; protection; and support, my family of a son; brother; cousin; uncle; nephew, and my community of a much needed leader.

I thought the life I had been living made me "the man" in my community, but in reality I was only partaking in my own self-destruction. And participating in the destruction of my community, making victims of my fellow human-beings. So it was imperative that I make the ultimate decision to completely change how I lived.

During this soul-searching undertaking of restaffing my think-tank, I discovered the healing power of forgiveness. Looking back, here I was in my early 30s, freshly sentenced to life, my heart filled with a lifetime of anger, resentment, bitterness, and frustration. I was resentful toward my biological father for not being in my life, heartbroken by the failed relationships with the mothers of my children, and beyond angered by the murder of so many family and friends. I wanted vengence on my enemies. I even had the audacity to be angered at the family of my victims for being angry at me for the pain and suffering I'd brought them through my senseless acts of violence.

I was done with it all! I was beyond weary of holding on to so much anger, and unforgiveness in my heart. It had all become so emotionally, mentally, and spiritually draining. I could no longer keep up with the facade of someone who had zero concern for the next person's well-being. So, I began the process of forgiveness, and that proved more difficult than changing the way I went about doing things. When you are wronged, or perceive what someone has done as wrong, it's human nature to harbor ill-feelings towards that person or those people. So I really had to dig deep if I had any hope of becoming the man I knew I was truly meant to be.

I began by first forgiving myself. I forgave myself for ever believing that showing emotion was weak, for thinking I had to behave a certain way to be accepted, for lying, cheating, and for stealing and robbing. I had to forgive myself for feeling I failed my children, their mothers, my family, my community, and my God. I forgave my father for never being part of my life, and for leaving me feeling abandoned. I forgave those I had previously considered enemies, and swore that it was "on sight" the next time we met.

I had even come face-to-face with sworn enemies, even family members of my victims, and was able to make amends with these people.

Its an indescribable feeling to be able to forgive and be forgiven for past offenses.

Walking through life not knowing where karma was coming from was too much to bare any longer. It was like the more I forgave the lighter my heart felt; the more mental, emotional, and spiritual freedom I experienced.

I am now going on 43 years old, and if you would've told me, in my late 20s or early 30s, that I would find freedom through the renewal of my thinking and forgiveness, I would've more than likely responded by saying that sounded like complete "SUCKA SHIT"! Now, I understand that renewed thinking and forgiveness is the mindset and characteristics of a changed and mature man.

All of my sons are now at the age of young men. And by the grace of God I've been able to maintain a close relationship with them all, my daughters included. Knowing first hand how easily a young man can be enticed by the fast-life or pressured into behaving in a way contrary to his true self, I often explain to them the difference between what the streets define as real man and what a real man is in reality.

Although many principles and morals are shared between the two, what ultimately seperates these two types of men is how they perceive the world around them. That is, false pride, misplaced honor, peer pressure, and ignorance.

I continue to ingrain in the minds of my children, and others I encounter, that the way you think determines your decisions and behavior. If you think positive, you make positive decisions, and behave in a positive manner, therefore, you lead a positive lifestyle.

It took me nearly four decades of self-imprisonment before reaching the degree of mental, emotional, and spiritual freedom I now live in today.

Brett Richardson
AL-4303

STEVE JENNINGS

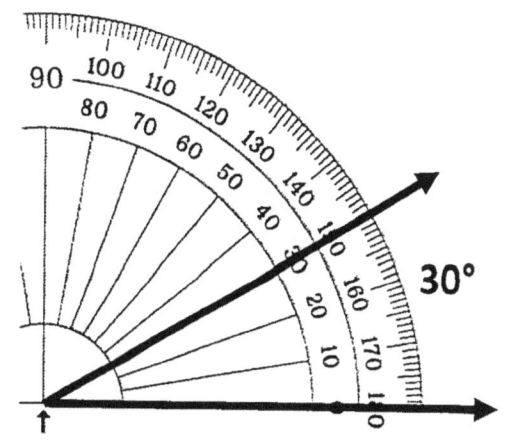

FIND NEW FRIENDS

Even in the Deepest of Depths

Our society here in the United States is the media's golden standard for civilized people to live in. Our officials even go abroad to help the "unadvanced" nations find the way. Yet, if you peer between the cracks, so many of our young men and women are regularly being displaced, left behind, victimized, devastated, and even discarded. My own experience is a story of missed opportunities that led to a tragic outcome for Greggory Garrett, his family, the community, and my own family.

During my formative years, I had all the hallmarks of continuing the cycle of drugs and violence. Growing up bouncing from one drug infested apartment complex to another, ambulances would wait until the cops would cuff and take away the suspect before helping the injured. Our safety, and well being, was second to getting the criminals under control. The only ones with nice cars, or enough food to actually eat three meals a day, were the ones settling for a life of criminal activities, drug sales, and violence.

Place a too young mother, with two young ones, by herself in this environment and you get me. I was the first born son to a father that wanted a thousand wives... well I exaggerate, but he has children with three women. My sister and I were on our own, just like our brother Micheal and his mother were, while our father found his "Leave it to Beaver" life with his wife and four youngest sons. My sister and I were often outside, or in our rooms, so Mom could fool herself into thinking we would not notice the drug transactions that brought in just enough food so we did not go without our three meals a day.

My male role models were maladjusted, abusive, or neglectful. One thing they all had in common was that they were only temporary. That is until my mother met my stepfather, who was too young to even have children when I was born. By the time I started school, the 'us against them' mentality was already beaten into my mind. School officials, and law enforcement, were only trying to get the 'us' people of our environment. Old convicts were all around, and friends were waiting for a parent to get home from prison.

By the time my mom found my stepfather I was nine years old, had been physically abused by her past boyfriends to "toughen me up", and had a strong distrust of the men in my life. My neighborhood was multicultural, yet the apartment complexes were either black, or a blend of white and Mexican. It was normal for all of the kids to blend together and play all day, then retreat to our separate complexes at night. The adults had conflicts along racial lines that would strain friendships, but it somehow worked in our corner of the world.

In the third grade, my cousins and I were split up to different schools. My sister, one cousin, and I were bussed to a "nice" school, while only my boy cousins got to stay in the school we all grew up going to. In this new environment, my constant fidgeting, and fascination for shiny things, became apparent. As a result, the school counselor suggested I be tested for a learning disability. My family saw this nosy interruption as a way of calling me stupid. The result of the tests was a referral to a doctor for a possible ADHD diagnosis. Barely getting by already, the family only saw more medical bills on top of the already stacking up emergency room visit bills from previous out of control behavior.

While the doctor diagnosed me with ADHD, my family diagnosed me as an 'outside kid' as the treatment would be too expensive. This is the first time that my mom got to hear the phrase, "He'll end up in prison if things don't change". How can school administrators say something like that, and not try to do something about it? I got to repeat the third grade, and was rewarded by going back to the school in the neighborhood away from nosy teachers. This was also the first time I was displaced from my peers. They went on to the fourth grade; moved up to the big kid playground while I struggled to sit still and blend in.

It was right around this time that Mom met my stepdad. After a loud, and long, night my sister and I woke up to a motorcycle in the living room, a guy sleeping on the coffee table, and a bunch of other people all over the apartment. The guy on the coffee table began to come over more and more often after that night, and eventually moved in with us. Weekends went from beer keg parties on our porch, to having to be home at eight o'clock sharp, and in bed by nine o'clock.

Now we were a two income family, and the rules increased as they planned for their wedding. I was eleven, and my stepdad was twenty-two. As he worked his way to becoming a machinist, we moved to the suburbs. Picket fence and all. Our street was a run down eyesore that the rest of this new neighborhood looked down on, but it was absolutely silent at night. No loud fights, and the cops were actually nice to people here.

Taken away from the friends I grew up with, and having a new disciplined life, church was also added in. We became devout Southern Baptists; present at church each time the doors were open. Our new neighborhood had rude parents:

blatantly pointing at us as the family that just moved in from a bad area, and that we were "poor people". In the ghetto we might not have had as many material possessions, but at least people weren't so rude. I fell in with the misfits of my peers.

The adjustment period was torture: being in class all day, then in church pews Sunday morning and nights, Wednesday nights, and every third Thursday. Just before Junior High began, we were returning from a summer rafting trip and noticed that fire trucks, an ambulance, and one or two sheriffs cars were on our street. Our neighbor had shot someone on his doorstep, and we were just in time to catch the clean up. To us, it was a surprise that only a couple cops showed up. To the parents of my (soon to be) Junior High classmates, it was proof that the people on our street were here to bring crime to their white utopia.

Most people would think that a young white kid would be at home in this (mostly) white neighborhood, but it was the exact opposite. I struggled to stay calm with my conditions, and keep my outbursts as appropriate as possible. I found my first savior, and first name brand item, when one of the older kids traded me his old skateboard for yard chores he no longer wanted to do. It also showed how little this neighborhood wanted us there. I was so proud of the brand on my skateboard that I took it everywhere; even school. I had to hide it in a bush during school because it was not allowed during school hours.

On the way home from school one day, I was talking to one of my classmates about where I skateboard. I had the board resting on my shoulder, holding the trucks, leaning it against the side of my head (I wanted everyone to see it was not generic) when my classmate's older sister began screaming for him to hurry up. The next morning the school was in a big buzz about a cop car being in the parking lot. We went to first period, and as class began the Principal and two officers entered the classroom. I was called to the back of the class, asked to open my locker, and then handcuffed. My introduction to handcuffs was humiliating, being in front of my entire class as they searched my locker. Escorted to the Principal's office, and on display, I found my classmate from the previous day crying next to his mother. As we waited for half-an-hour (which seemed like ten years) for my mother to arrive from work, I finally found out why the classmate's sister was screaming to him to hurry up. The previous day, it had been reported that I was threatening him with my skateboard. My mother was in utter dismay that I was in handcuffs, and I was finally released when she arrived. The young classmate was adamant that I never threatened him, but I was still suspended. I was relieved I was not arrested, but my skateboard in the bushes was still against the rules.

This showed me that the childhood 'us vs. them' was still real. I didn't mind being in trouble though. I got to spend time alone with mom, and pick up my sister when her day ended. I loved that selfish moment of it being just the three of us again. Step-Pop came home with all of his rules though, and I was apparently just a bad kid. All my fidgeting at school, and now cops calling Mom to pick me up. I found out from Pop that I was a 'burn out' kid. Apparently, in the seventh grade I was already into drugs before I had even experimented. During a family counseling session Pop disappeared, and later a phone call revealed that he was at home searching my room. No drugs; but he found a page torn out of a pornographic magazine inside of an encyclopedia, and it was very graphic.

Reinforcing my distrust, my stubborn will kicked in, and now I went on the offensive. While spending the night at a friend's house that was struggling to understand his parent's divorce, we spent our allowance on some weed from his older neighbor. We weren't cool enough to smoke it with him, but he bent up a soda can, poked some holes in it, then sent us on our merry way.

My first high was mostly giggling at the dogs, and asking if I was actually high. It was all it took though to introduce me to a life of addiction. This overwhelmed my stepfather, who was tired of my grandparents advice. I soon found out my grandfather did as well. My grandma was the only one to give consideration to, or believe in, my ADHD. My grandfather was hatching a plan, however.

Being back in the neighborhood I grew up in, I was desperate to reconnect and fit back in. All my friend's parents were still struggling with addictions, and criminality. I was now the kid whose family was too good for them. Lucky for me, there were no rules again, and we were sneaking alcohol, and smoking cigarettes and weed. Then, one of my friends stole a coffee can full of change from my grandfather's room.

Meanwhile, my grandparents had planned a vacation. Grandma would fly down to my aunt's house, and grandpa would get there later. Confusing plans until grandpa got back from dropping grandma off at the airport. It was at this time that grandpa revealed (in so many words) that he had raised all of his kids, and was done with children. So, I could go run around with my friends, or go home to my mommy.

Well, since ya put it that way! I grabbed my backpack, stuffed it with everything I owned, and decided I was a grown ass man right there on the spot. That night (with a group of my "runaway" friends) my buddy's older brother taught me not only how to drive, but also how to steal a car. I was a real criminal now. All of fourteen years old, and I had already learned all I needed to know to be an adult somehow.

Another desperate soul I knew had lost his mother to the prison system, so we took over the rent. A couple fourteen-year-olds, and a few other teens. Out of the five of us, not one was eighteen yet. Of them, I was supposed to be the one who had a hope, so the older two of my roommates made sure that I was at school for the beginning of my eighth grade year. This was going well until rumor of my "living" at my grandparent's house (outside of the district) reached the Principal. I had been falling asleep in classes, suspended for horseplay, and disrupting class by the second semester. Each time I got in trouble my mom, or grandma, would pick me up from school. I got to spend time with them, eat good; then back off to my "runaway kids" crowd.

There were times that I did go "home to mommy" (as the men in my life called it) but only in bursts. The Principal eventually acted on the rumors of not living at my parent's house. First the standard locker search, then a meeting. Instead of mentioning that I was struggling, and half-ass living on my own, to the appropriate authorities, I was expelled from the "nice" school for having trace amounts of tobacco in a pouch of my backpack.

This was proof to me that the "adults" in the room were useless, and reinforced my bad behavior. Any one reading this can see that I only needed to be honest to get help, but I was a fourteen year old adult! I could have even gone home and obeyed the rules, learned to express myself correctly, and lived the humble (safe) life that my stepfather was struggling to provide. Again, just another example of an opportunity blown off because I loved the excitement of living with no rules. Sneaking into cars and stealing them; the 'we' mentality of the gang lifestyle was setting in. I was absolutely desperate to fit in, and on my way to a long struggle with grief.

Not able to go back to the "nice" school, my grandparents enrolled me in the Junior High in our neighborhood. My reputation of running around with the "runaway crowd", stealing cars, and even getting into fights with other gang members was already well known to the kids I grew up with. Unfortunately, the kids I grew up with were already at the school in our neighborhood. On my first day on the bus to school, it was pointed out that only six white boys attended this 'pee-wee Blood' school. I didn't feel threatened though. I had grown up with these guys. Even the young Bloods told me this.

My first day of school back in the neighborhood would not be a positive experience. The first bell did not mean 'go to class'. Instead it meant 'jump the white boy because he's in some other gang'. I pretended that my friends and I were not a gang, but when you participate in gang activity, other gangs take notice. School officials broke up the no-injury fight. I did not hurt anybody (I was taller and larger than nearly all of the other students), but honestly, we were all just children to mimic the older guys.

In the Principal's office, the Principal decided that everyone's silence meant that I must have used a racial slur on the bus before school. Now, I was apparently a teen racist, waiting for someone to pick me up from school. Call me what you want though, I was going to get to hang out with my grandma, or mom, and eat a good meal. This was my perception of consequences. I received a zero-tolerance expulsion for five minutes of madness, and became a Junior High drop out.

Having proven that I do not talk to authority, I found a perverted sense of respect amongst my criminal peers. I also found out how expendable criminals really are. One night, while trying to steal a car, my friend Miguel was shot with a shotgun slug by the home owner. Then, a few days later the two older friends in our apartment were arrested. Down to just three of us now, it was time to kick it in to high gear to afford our rent. We decided to go get that home owner that shot Miguel that only went to jail for three hours before being release to brag to the media.

Fortunately, the police officers kicked up patrols in front of the home owner's street. We would have stolen a car in broad daylight at a parking lot if they weren't. But that guy was big, and the cops were all over. Better yet, with all of the extra running around I got sick; strep throat and bronchitis. Dehydrated and struggling to breathe, one of my last friends dumped me off at my mom's house. Back to the suburbs!

Another missed opportunity. It was the end of summer, and I was back at Mom's. I was enrolled at the high school by her house. At least it was the one I chose at a mock career day in the seventh grade, before things went off track. I even made the football team. I went from criminal, to jock, just like that. I quit smoking because I needed my wind. Now healthy, in a heartbeat

I found my next, worst enemy. While on my own, there had been encounters with promiscuous girls, and unsafe sex. Now as a football player though, they were everywhere.

Back at home, two parents working meant I had way too much time alone. My sister (who I dearly missed) and I would have friends over each day that would scatter at the sound of parent's cars coming home. The girls in this neighborhood were mostly latch-key kids as well. I began to adopt my birth father's idea of love, by using young women to prove that I was a man. My relationships were all based on whether we were having sex or not, with no understanding of the emotions tied in. I was grieving for my friends. One dead; two arrested.

The next conflict with my Pop proved to be too much for my mom. When things became overwhelming, and talk of sending me away again came up, Mom's marriage ended. There were other circumstances that contributed to their divorce as well, but a fifteen year-old mind only felt guilt for ruining everything again. Soon after, the stress boiled over in my mom, so she did a lot of yelling about me being just like my birth father, and added the responsibility for destroying her marriage. Placed in this situation, I wanted to go back to my friends, but felt too guilty for destroying Mom's life again. First, by being conceived, and now by running her husband off. Even worse, my sister missed Pop, and started to act out as well.

All the freedom of High School, and the lack of supervision, proved to be too much. I started skipping classes with my new friends and the young women from school. Drinking from liquor cabinets, smoking weed, popping pills in the medicine cabinets, and all the promiscuous girls became the only focus in my life. Football took a back seat. Then, one day, an even worse thing happened. Already mad that I was popping up with a new T.V., VCR, and stereo equipment, Mom had caught me weighing out bags of weed to take to school. Her first reaction was, "don't sell that shit out of my house". Then, as she was walking away, over her shoulder she asked me to roll a joint and smoke it with her.

While still struggling with girls, drugs, and fitting in after losing my old friends, I found the next school official who cared enough to notice. The Principal called me to the office for a parent-Principal conference. After assuring me that I was not 'technically' in trouble, he let me know that he recognized that I needed help. The grade check requirement to play football revealed that I was behind on my grades, and missing classes. He suggested a smaller environment; the continuation school. I had destroyed my opportunity to continue in sports, and found myself in the misfit school.

This was yet another opportunity that I threw away. The closer attention helped me at first, then it got out that my friends were welcome to drink, and do drugs, at my house openly. A few months into this misfit school and I already found my way to being involved in casual relationships with some of the young women in this micro-environment as well. I found a way to advance my addictions.

Soon I met some students at the continuation school that lived in a co-ed group home. Some of the girls there were struggling to understand their past of drugs, and sexual abuse, in the foster care system. At lunch, two of these lost souls introduced me to crystal meth. Up to this point, I had only seen tweekers and thought they were weird. I had never tried it myself. With the temptation to prove that I was a grown man to these struggling ladies, I jumped in. If I had to do the drugs to get in; my house was unsupervised, and I was willing. It was immediately apparent to me that these "women" were still girls. They might have been a couple years older than me, but even my first time being high on meth, I noticed something strange about the encounter.

My teen years continued along this line. I spoiled many opportunities from this point on, and slipped through the cracks as well. I found ways to just blend into whatever environment I found myself in. I returned to my neighborhood after my mom got evicted due to all of the teens hanging out there. This time, I overcompensated for having retreated back to the suburbs. My return to my old neighborhood became violent and excessive. I escalated my drug use, learned to sell drugs to support my habit, and spread this disease to any peer around me.

One of the worst things that could have happened came upon my return to the neighborhood. I met my "real" father, and my four half-brothers. In my mind, he had moved on with his new family. Being around them made me feel discarded, and thrown away. My drug use became even worse. I was now too dangerous to be around my half-brothers.

The lifestyle cost more friends jail time, and a couple more their lives. Each time, instead of recognizing the precious gift of life and freedom, I only recognized how expendable we truly were. Living to age eighteen did not seem likely. All the male role models in my life spoke of how "when" I got to prison, I would see all of my friends. There was no "if" with how we acted. My actions were becoming bolder and bolder; to prove I belonged in the hood. I began to agree with my "role models": If I made it to prison before I was put in a box, it would be a great reunion with my friends.

As my life was spiralling down the criminality drain, my sister and mom were loving comfortably, remarried to Pop. Just as I was feeling sorry for myself, and completely isolated from my family, I got sick again. Chicken pox at seventeen was no fun at all. I lost everything I had hustled for because I was too sick to support myself.

With my last couple of dollars in my pocket, ready to beg a desperate single mother to let me sleep on her couch, my Pop showed up out of nowhere. I had no clue (and still don't know) how he knew where to find me. But here would be the biggest opportunity I would flush down the toilet.

Pop told me to come home and heal with the family, even after all of the drama I had caused; refusing to just be a kid and be taken care of through my teen years. Two weeks later I turned eighteen. I was still drinking, and smoking cigarettes and weed with my family, but I also had two weeks clean from meth. The help did not end with a home either. Pop helped me get a job where he worked - building military equipment. I had full medical, dental, and life insurance, and had a 401k plan at eighteen years-old.

Smart people would have realized the perks, and put their noses to the grindstone. We were a happy family until my little sister (still in her rebellious period) continued to run away. Pop co-signed a lease for me, so I could rent a one bedroom apartment. At work we had as much overtime as we could handle. I worked my way to 'welding apprentice', working the hardest metal to weld: three inch aluminum.

With all the overtime, a few of us started using meth like it was a tool in our tool box, and could be controlled. Overtime was constant. A few months in, I started shutting down on Sunday morning, and not waking up on time for my shift on Monday because I was so exhausted.

Lack of sleep, paired with being amped up on meth, led to an aggressive argument with a co-worker. Stack this with my not showing up on time for a couple Mondays in a row, and I was put on probation. Being an adult, it was my responsibility to recognize that meth was not a tool to help me work my overtime. One day, I came home from work to find my apartment emptied of all appliances. The reformed car thief had his apartment burglarized. I was so mad that I would have regretted anything I would have done if I had caught who did it. Then, an old friend called, was in trouble, and needed help.

While selling large amounts of crystal meth, someone had robbed him. This needed to be addressed before everyone thought they could steal from him as well. I felt obligated. This was one of the friends who had helped me at fourteen, when I was homeless. One night back in the neighborhood would go from excessively violent, to excessive drug use, to promiscuousness, to two weeks of excess. We got his drug stash, and money (and some extra), back and immediately went on a binge. This binge destroyed the last fifteen months of hard work, and help from my family. My job was gone, and the apartment directly after. Everything Pop helped me with I had thrown away.

Utter failure helps some see rock bottom. I embraced, and wallowed in it. Immediately accepting my expendability again, and desperate to prove I would never leave our little ghetto every again, I became the first to help any friend in any violent way. The last nine months of my freedom would be a drug, and alcohol, filled binge so thick that it would take dynamite to get through to my brain. The shame kept me from even looking in my family's direction for any reason.

This is where I would destroy two families for eternity. Desperate now to prove that I was the most down, and in this for life, I escalated a simple disagreement into a murder. It was not even my dispute to settle. So desperate was I to prove that I would protect any friend that accepted me, and that I feared no man, Greggory Garrett would lose his life.

I would pay for this crime with a twenty-to-life sentence for second degree murder. Still refusing to recognize all the devastation I caused, I dove in to prison life head first. I accepted all the other desperate and maladjusted peers as brothers-in-arms. Learning that, as a good white man, it was my duty to "earn" my bed (and still desperate to fit in with a hunger for power and control), I now accepted the White Supremist agenda without even finding out why whites were supposedly so much better than every other race. I was so happy to be accepted that the cops had to tell me to stop smiling after my first assault that earned me my bed.

Soon it became apparent that all these fearless killers I looked up to, and hoped to be accepted by, were not as fearless as they pretended to be. One thing they had in common was that they were terrified of blemishing their personas by losing a fight. Having grown up being beaten by some of my mom's old boyfriends, that fear was gone for me. From my perspective, there were cops everywhere to break it up anyway. So, I learned to be explosively violent at the first sign of aggression.

Just to make things even more hopeless, I discovered the perverted path to honor in the skinhead movement. The more hopeless, violent, and maladjusted, the higher the honor. Within five years in prison, I was already involved in several batteries (some with weapons), making the cops pull me out of my cell while violently resisting numerous times, three race riots, and (most of all) surviving the dreaded Security Housing Unit (SHU). I had proven myself.

Being a full fledged gang member, even superior to others, I was finally someone. Everytime I felt my peers becoming too close, I would assault someone to go somewhere else. When I would arrive on a new yard, my presence was celebrated. I now had power, and control. I found my way to being the best failure amongst all these failures. Now my actions came to be noticed; gaining me favor amongst the prison gangs.

When normal people hear the name 'Aryan Brotherhood', most immediately recoil from the stereotype alone. In prison they are worshipped, and honored, as the absolute power amongst white prisoners. My (so-called) missions, or work, up to this point were all labeled 'hard targets'. It is not pretty when a tank full of sharks turn on one another, just to prove they will survive as the fittest. The white group yards in Administrative Segregation (Ad-Seg) often looked as if there were numerous shark attacks at the end of most yard periods.

Up to this point, I had accepted this lifestyle as what I was born for. I began to realize that none of the (dreamt of) big reunions with friends from the streets were happening. To be honest, none of the tough convicts I looked up to were on the shark tank yards I always landed on. They were actually whino-time, lower-level lames. Here I was, having put in ten times the work, from ages nineteen to twenty-nine, and I had more influence than every one of them.

While I was "working" my way up the food chain, I was given my chance to prove that I could run a yard after leaving the dreaded Pelican Bay SHU. I showed that I could tell a person, with multiple murders, to get a knife so we could stab one another to settle a dispute. I was now 'cream of the crop'; so naturally it was my time to graduate from manipulated to manipulator.

Then, I finally got to have one of those reunions I was told would happen. One of the guys from the neighborhood, who claimed me as his nephew, showed up. Old, and barely able to get out of his wheelchair; here was a glimpse of my future in prison. My conscience was starting to work against me as well.

Prison politics for whites were a path of proving who was the biggest killer. If a serial murderer comes to prison, we try to kill him for being a weirdo. Yet, if a person kills multiple people within prison, he becomes a prime candidate for the Aryan Brotherhood. If a white is afraid, or shows fear, they become prey. Developing a moral compass is even worse.

Two things happened while I was a "shot caller" on one of the yards at one of the worst prisons in California. First, I was introduced to 'Restorative Justice' programs. Second, one of my associates was murdered on one of the other yards. He was killed because he refused to attack another inmate with a weapon, and so that one of the other shot callers could prove he was not afraid of my affiliate to our superiors. It ended badly for the person he asked to carry out the attack, and he basically sold his soldier out. This was another reminder of how expendable, and worthless, our lives were by our own standards.

I thank The Creator for the next turn of events. Before I became responsible for another lost life, or took another myself, I was validated as a prison gang associate. This removed me from General Population, and isolated me; giving me time to think about my current circumstances. Taking that long, hard, look in the mirror was my wake-up call. The motto of 'Restorative Justice', "it is never too late to become a good person", finally kicked in.

I was finally finding ways to be accountable for my actions. Turning my back on my nasty associates, I walked away from my gang as well. I started learning how to be responsible for myself, and become a productive person. Through N.A. (Narcotics Anonymous) I found sobriety, and a debt that I owed to society. Beginning to learn the reasons that I used drugs led to insight into a log of my old behavior.

As a young person, I allowed myself to be manipulated into most of the situations I found myself in. By accepting the stubborn mentality of not asking for help at a young age, I robbed myself of so many opportunities. By not trying to understand and overcome the abuse I suffered as a child, I shut down and even became abusive to my peers. My abandonment issues stemmed from seeking approval from maladjusted adults that were always temporary in my life. The people who tried to help me (like my stepfather, the high school Principal, and my supervisors at work) I distrusted, because my self-esteem was so low that I felt I did not deserve a chance.

Robbing myself of opportunities amplified my failures, and contributed to my drug addictions. I felt so low because I refused to accept opportunity. I could not understand, or accept, why someone would want me around unless we were using drugs together. The shame and sadness from losing the job my Pop gave me only amplified my addictions. Going back to my old neighborhood that final time, I had become so desperate to fit in that no amount of violence was off the table.

My most shameful action though, was that I was more concerned about my ego than Greg's life. I murdered a man because I was more afraid of one of my older associates saying I was not down for my homies than I was of prison, becoming a murderer, or having any regard for Greg's life, or family. I could swear to being manipulated into this state of mind, but I accepted being manipulated when all truth is told.

Coming to accept some hard truth was the only way of accepting responsibility for my past. At first the emotions were overwhelming. I found relief by pledging to never harm another person, and the longer this went on the better I began to feel. Learning the way of making amends (an N.A. and A.A. necessity) it became apparent that I need to show kindness to every person I come in contact with as recompense for the kindness that I stole from the world when I became a murderer.

No longer using violence to back up all my communication, I had to learn new ways of interacting with people. Learning assertive, non-aggressive, communication was a new experience at the age of thirty-five. Gaining insight into my past helped me find more character defects that needed to be fixed.

Eventually, maintaining my new (kinder) way of life started becoming a struggle. Learning about spirituality became my step two. Maintaining closer contact with my higher power became a point of contention, however. Before my recovery, I was involved in Odinism: a nature based religion, where we celebrate the contributions of our ancestors, and are obligated to leave a contribution to our descendants for them to honor us for. The problem with this religion for me was that the skinhead movement had perverted much of it into a racially exclusive way of living, and I had contributed to this perversion as a gang member.

I found my way home when discussions with one of my Native American friends led to conversations about his way of life. Learning about the purification ceremonies of the Lakota Peoples led me towards much healing. I was invited to a "guest sweat". In preparation for this, I focused on giving all of my resentments, and violent character flaws, to the rocks; opening myself up so the Creator could bring me peace and balance; allowing the Spirit World to guide me in a positive direction.

This opportunity helped me to forgive myself for all of the opportunities that I had robbed myself of. I also began to forgive myself for all of the violence I committed that had hardened my soul. I have opened myself up to finding ways to seek forgiveness from those I have harmed in my past, where the opportunity has presented itself.

Learning more of this way of life has motivated a search for a better lifestyle by walking the 'Red Road' as a 'Seventh Generation Practitioner'. It was told by many strong elders that the Seventh Generation will be the one to bring back the way of the People as one tribe. Having a closer contact with my spirituality, and the forgiving ways of the People, has allowed me to flourish.

The opportunity to stay with the physical manifestations of suffering for what I need, instead of what I want, has brought so much healing and peace to me. I've grown leaps and bounds. Now I am able to embrace love, and truly live as the better person that I am now. There is still a massive amount of hurt, pain, and sorrow that I must make up for. I will continue to seek solutions as I commune with the Spirit World, and be open to them when Grandfather gives the opportunities to me.

Being one with everything around me keeps me mindful of my attitude, and actions. Every living being has a connection, as we are all relatives in the Creator's eyes. Through this moral framework, race relations became opportunities to learn more about other people's way of life instead of looking for ways of standing apart. I am now able to celebrate cultural differences, and embrace each person in my path, as friends.

At this point, I am waiting for my third chance of proving I have earned my freedom. As a person who has cut short a precious life, I do not deserve, nor is there any obligation that I be released from prison. Embracing my recovery, and being a better person, is my obligation. The debt I incurred by taking a life made it my responsibility to show kindness, for the kindness I robbed the community of.

When many Lifers go to their parole hearings, they show a great amount of empathy for the victim, and family, they harmed. When a life is stolen though, it is not just the individual and family that suffer, but the community as well. Consider all of the people that a single person comes into contact with in their lifetime. Now imagine robbing each of those people of their safety, peace of mind, all of the positive contact with the individual, as well as the love. That is the debt a murderer owes to the universe.

Just because I allowed myself to lose my self-esteem, and gave my choices over to a gang as a result, doesn't mean that I am not accountable for all of the harm I created. We are not born good or bad; our choices decide if we are good or bad. Coming from a negative, and volatile, environment does not make a person expendable, or bad. Settling for a life of being manipulated and negative is a choice. There were many opportunities where I could have chose to ask for help, and risen above just settling for trash. It is so simple to accept our failures and give up. It is also simple to stop being an ass, show some humility, and find the help needed to overcome, and learn from, our failures. To walk around without having a higher power leaves a person open to an endless amount of negative, and selfish choices.

I hope to be an example that it really is never too late to fix your life. Society requires us to be better people. At no time are we forceably trapped into a negative lifestyle. There are recovery communities waiting to help. All a person needs to do is act on the desire. No matter how hopeless life seems to be, there is always a light waiting to be approached. To all my newfound relatives who are struggling: there are those of us who have clawed our way out of the deepest of depths, just waiting to help you find your way. All you have to do is ask. Help can be found no matter how low you are feeling. Just choose to overcome rather than choosing to settle. Either way, it is a choice left for each and every one of us.

To all my relations,
Steve J. Jennings
J85853

JOSE DUARTE

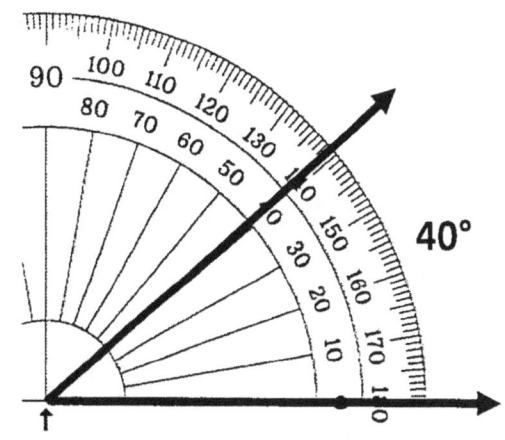

PLAN FOR SUCCESS

Turning Obstacles into Opportunities

All journey's begin in wonder. Any step toward your destination may seem daunting if the path is long and difficult. Many aspects must be considered, and much forethought is required, to execute a well thought out plan of traveling hundreds of miles: traversing dangerous and steep mountainsides, forging new paths in overgrown open valleys, overcoming dehydration, starvation, and imposing one's will to survive when nature is dangerous and unpredictable. In order for me to understand the origin of that which galvanized me to take that all-important first step on my college journey, I needed to delve into my past, as well as that of my father's.

Before immigrating, my father contemplated foregoing the many days of difficult travel required, and remaining in his homeland of Mexico. The comforts he enjoyed their were minimal, yet known and predictable. As predictable as the sun rising each morning and fading in the evening. Ultimately though, he knew his heart would be unsettled if he never took the all-important first step towards America.

Like most immigrants before him, his desire to leave his homeland was based on opportunity and a dream. He rightfully believed that the United States of America was a land of plenty that could afford him, and his future progeny, success. Of course, this was possible if focus, hardwork, and determination was exerted. Then, that dream may be manifest into a reality.

So, he charted his course that began in Sinaloa, Mexico and ended in Los Angeles, California. With a backpack filled with amenities, a pocket full of currency, and a younger brother for company, he took his first step on an arduous path. He began each day more tired than the last, and ended them praying to the stars that dotted the night sky that his motivation wouldn't waver. His cause was to invest in his, and his children's, future. Nothing less would suffice.

From under a canopy of trees, to the wide open plains of the valley, his trek proceeded. He had reached mountain tops and stopped to admire the view but for the briefest of moments because his goal was set, his target defined. Even with days of hunger and thirst, he was determined. With each laborious step, he maintained his persistence. With each injurious mile, he persevered. But what was the driving force that propelled him beyond the aspirational standard of parents wanting their children to have a good future? A distinguishing characteristic of my father was his ambition. 'Settling' was not a word in his vocabulary. He took great pride in striving toward the better qualities in life. He'll never admit as much however, because perpetual elevation is his standard.

Constant ascension is not a fixed state, it is in motion at all times. A worthy quality indeed, if harnessed delicately and taught correctly. His intentions were good, but his belief required refinement. We can climb mountains to escape dangers such as: cliffs, lack of proper shelter, scarce food, limited water supply, and much more. This is to say that there is more to life than to focus only on one aspect of it. My father erroneously believed that coming to America, obtaining an income, and having children on fertile grounds was the end of his journey. My errors in my life are mine to own; however, they are a bi-product of my father's journey being half-fulfilled.

Research has found that people at every age are social and active, not just reactive. Instead of responding merely to their own direct experiences, "People act on the environment. They create it, preserve it, transform it, and even destroy it... in a socially embedded interplay" (Bandura, 2006, p. 167). That social interplay is the foundation of social learning theory, which holds that humans sometimes learn without personal reinforcement. As the primary proponent of this theory, Albert Bandura explains that this learning often occurs through 'modeling' (people copying what they see others do; also observational learning) (Bandura, 1986, 1997). Modeling is not simply imitation: some people are more likely to follow, or be, role models than others. Of course, people model only some actions, of some individuals, in some contexts. Sometimes people do the opposite of what they have seen. Generally speaking, modeling is most likely when the observer (me) is uncertain or inexperienced, and when the model(s) are admired, powerful, nurturing, or similar to the observer. This explains why modeling is especially powerful in childhood, and why parents and/or relatives are such powerful models.

With modeling in mind, it's clear that my initial behaviors were formed without much forethought or understanding behind my decisions that did so. They weren't deliberate or calculated. "Do as I say not as I do" was an old phrase I heard often as a child. Usually after I'd witnessed such bad habits as: drug and/or alcohol abuse, use of tobacco products, lying, cheating, irresponsibility, or violence. My parents had no clue that I was modeling behaviors that they were exhibiting, yet much as I want to cry foul for the way I was molded, I am reminded that life is one big journey; not a destination.

My father's destination was America. However, he should not have overlooked his incomplete personal journey. I was a man-in-training, and it was his filial responsibility to raise me as such. To guide me into a responsible human being. To teach me values, ethics, and the roles expected of me. He didn't know how to however, therefore I didn't learn, which stunted my development in many ways. My father had reached his destination and acted as if the journey was over. Our journey's are never over once we make it to a destination though. Life's destination's should only serve as rest stops.

According to American behavioral psychologist, John B. Watson, every behavior is, and can be, learned. He wrote, "Give me a dozen healthy infants, well-informed, and my own specified world to bring them up in, and I'll guarantee to take any one at random and train him to become any type of specialist I might select - doctor, lawyer artist, merchant chief, and yes, even beggar-man and thief - regardless of his talents, penchants, tendencies, abilities, vocations, and race of his ancestors." Behavioral learning is far more comprehensive than the narrow definition of learning that focuses on academic knowledge. Instead, for behaviorists, everything that people do, and feel, is learned. For example, newborns need to learn to suck on a nipple; infants need to learn motor skills; preschoolers need to learn to hold hands when crossing the street; adults need to learn how to budget time and money.

The most influential North American proponent of behaviorism was B.F. Skinner. His most famous contribution was to recognize another type of conditioning - operant conditioning (also called instrumental conditioning) - in which animals (including people) act, and then something follows that action. In other words, Skinner went beyond learning by association, in which one stimulus is paired with another stimulus (as in Ivan Pavlov's experiment on dog saliva, where he paired an audible tone with feeding time). Skinner focused on what happens after a behavior elicits a particular response. If the consequence that follows is enjoyable, the person tends to repeat the behavior; if the consequence is unpleasant, the person does not do that action again. Consequences that increase the frequency, or strength, or a particular action are called reinforcers, in a process called reinforcement. The true test is the effect a consequence has on the individual's future actions, not whether it is intended to be reward or punishment. A child, or an adult, who repeats an offense may have been reinforced, not punished, for the first action. As a whole, behavioral psychology helps us to understand why it is we conduct ourselves a certain way, and how our habits are formed.

During the 1990s, I witnessed gangs in my neighborhood, drug dealers, drug abuse, and violence. Without a father to give me the proper guidance to becoming a man, I did what was natural in my circumstances and learned from the streets instead. By way of operant conditioning I learned that when disrespected, harmed, or ridiculed, I had to act violently to receive a "kudos"; a well-done. This praise made me feel good, boosting my self-esteem, and became the reinforcement that led me to develop a violent nature. My cohorts dealt with the same circumstances, and at that time it was my culture; the culture of the underworld. It's all I knew. Frederick Douglass said, "A man's character always takes it's hue from the form and color of things about him". And man was he correct! Little did I know that the winds of time, and the tide of circumstance, were shaping me in ways that I didn't understand.

Take, for example, a person with high-reactive temperament. This person will have a higher heart rate, more widely dilated pupils, tighter vocal chords, and more cortisol (a stress hormone) in their saliva. They are more likely to feel jangled when they confront something new and stimulating. This type of person seems internally fragile. One can only imagine their susceptibility to mental, emotional, and physical decline when they are exposed to struggles of their era, such as: violence (domestic or otherwise), drug use and/or abuse, crime, gangs, instability, insecurity, and lack of positive role models. According to a groundbreaking theory dubbed "The Orchid Hypothesis" by David Dobbs, many children are like dandelions; able to thrive in just about any environment. Others, however, including the high-reactive types, are more like orchids: they wilt easily, but can grow strong and magnificent under the right conditions.

It wasn't until I learned about high-reactive types that I identified with those physical responses to adverse childhood events. My environment was not conducive to growth. My environment caused me stress for prolonged periods, causing that stress to be toxic. Needless to say, whatever talents that I may have possessed were not cultivated, and (as a seed planted in terrible soil) I did not grow strong and magnificent. I wilted.

One way to view how a person would further their development via the streets is to look through the lense of Sociocultural theorist. One hallmark of newer theories is that they are decidedly multicultural; influenced by the growing awareness that cultures shape experiences and attitudes. Some cultural differences within the United States arise from ethnic and national origins, some from socioeconomic status, and some are related to region, age, and gender. The central thesis of sociocultural theory is that human development results from the dynamic interaction between developing persons and their

surrounding society. Culture is not something external that encroaches on
developing persons. It is instead something that is internalized; integral
to everyday attitudes and actions.

The pioneer of the sociocultural perspective was a psychologist named
Lev Vygotsky. In his view, each person (schooled or not) develops with the
guidance of more skilled members of his or her society. Those people become
tutors, or mentors, in an "apprenticeship in thinking". Vygotsky believed
that children become apprentices to adults who teach them how to think by
explaining ideas, asking questions, and repeating values. He developed the
concept "guided participation", the method used by parents, teachers, and
entire societies to teach their novices the skills and habits expected within
their culture.

To describe this process, tutors engage learners (apprenticed) on joint
activities, offering "mutual involvement in several widespread cultural practices
with great importance for learning: narratives, routines, and play". During
a childs development it becomes crucial that the role model/tutor is positive,
and guides their apprentice into becoming an asset to their family, community,
and to the world. This responsibility is more than a filial duty. It is a
moral obligation in developing and guiding any young and impressionable person
to emerge as a decent human being. Failure to heed this (to borrow the metaphorical
"Orchid" again) obscures the light of the sun that is attempting to nourish
the plant reaching toward it.

I was born during the drug epidemic in the 1980's, which landed my formative
years in the crime surging 1990's. My single mother raised me while battling
a myriad of struggles including (but not limited to) mental health, and drug
and alcohol addictions. In my home, I had no guided participation because
there were no positive role-models available. The streets welcomed me with
arms wide open.

They offered mentor substitutes in older teenagers who would show us
the way when adults could, and did, not. I learned to lie and manipulate.
I had to. Others were conspiring to do the same all around me, so (the logic
went) if I did so first, I would not be the fool. I was taught to steal if
I couldn't afford to get what I desired. I was taught to fight others to show
my toughness. I was taught to evade accountability and responsibility related
to wrong-doings, or crime. Of course, after displaying these behaviors I would
be given some form of reinforcement: a pat on the back, a high-five, being
asked to join familial events, and/or a look of admiration or respect. This

conditioning shaped the landscape of my adolescence.

    Habits were all that mattered. After all, to think about my actions would cause hesitancy, and hesitancy is kryptonite to the impulsivity that led to the superficial love I received outside of my home. Living in a very dysfunctional home is like planting a seed in sand, not watering it, not giving it sunlight, and then wondering why a healthy plant doesn't grow. According to the Orchid Hypothesis (posited earlier by David Dobbs), these conditions are not environmental factors ideal for growth, but contributes moreso to a life of failure. There is a cure to the disease of failure, however; education. While on my educational journey, I have found remedies to the toxins that stunted my early growth, allowing me to find freedom.

    A seafarer does not travel on open waters without some form of navigation system. He uses a compass to help in the direction he wishes to travel. It is what guides him to the safety of land. As with the seafarer, man needs a moral compass to guide his conduct amongst others or risk being relegated to an untamed beast: dangerous and kept at bay. Morality is, at the very least, the effort to guide one's conduct by reason while giving equal weight to the interests of each individual affected by one's actions, painting the picture of what it means to be a conscientious moral agent. The conscientious moral agent is someone who:

(1) Is concerned impartially with the interests of everyone affected by what he or she does.
(2) Carefully sifts facts and examines their implications.
(3) Accepts principles of conduct only after scrutinizing them to make sure they are justified.
(4) Will "listen to reason" even when it means revising prior convictions.
(5) Is willing to act on these deliberations.

    Thomas Hobbes, the leading British philosopher of the 17th century, tried to show that morality does not depend on appealing to a god to issue commands and reward virtue. Instead, Hobbes believed morality should be understood as the solution to a practical problem that arises for self-interested human beings. We all want to live as well as possible, but in order to flourish we need a peaceful and cooperative social order, and we cannot have one without rules. Supposing there were no government institutions - no laws, police, or courts. What would it be like if there were no way to enforce social rules? We would be free to do as we pleased; what Hobbes called "the state of nature".

In the state of nature, he says, there would be no place for industry because the fruit thereof is uncertain; and consequently no culture of the earth; no navigation nor use of the commodities that may be imported by sea; no commodius building; no instruments of moving, and removing; no knowledge of the face of the earth; no account of time; no arts; no society; and worst of all, continual fear and danger of violent death. The life of man would be solitary, poor, nasty, and brutish.

Hobbes believed the state of nature would be awful due to four facts about human life:

(1) There is equality of need.
(2) There is scarcity.
(3) There is the essential equality of human power.
(4) There is limited altruism.

Together, these facts paint a grim picture. All needing the same basic things, and not enough of them to go around. Therefore, we would all have to compete for them. The result is a constant state of war of one with all. Life in the state of nature would be intolerable.

To escape the state of nature, we must find a way to work together. People must agree on rules to govern their interactions. They must agree, for example, not to harm one another and not to break their promises. Hobbes calls such an agreement "the social contract". As a society, we follow certain rules, and we have ways to enforce them. Some of those ways involve the law - if you assault someone, the police may arrest you. Other ways involve "the court of public opinion" - if you get a reputation for lying, then people may turn their backs on you. In the state of nature, it is every man for himself. But in society, altruism becomes possible. By releasing us from "the continual fear of violent death", the social contract frees us to take heed of others.

Jean-Jacques Rousseau went so far as to say that we become different kinds of creatures when we enter civilized relations with others. In the 'Social Contract', he writes,

> "The passage from the state of nature to the civil state produces a very remarkable change in man... Then only, when the voice of duty takes the place of physical impulses... does man, who so far had considered only himself, find that he is forced to act on different principles, and to consult

> his reason before listening to his inclinations... His faculties
> are so stimulated and developed... his being so ennobled,
> and his whole soul uplifted that, did not the abuses of this
> new condition often degrade him below the which he left,
> he would be bound to bless continually the happy moment which
> took him from it forever, and, instead of a stupid and unimagin-
> ative animal, made him an intelligent being and a man."

And what does the "voice of duty" require this new man to do? It requires him to set aside his self-centered designs in favor of rules that benefit everyone.

During the summer of 2011, while in administrative segregation for demonstrating a propensity for violence, I layed on my metal bunk and contemplated that requirement; that voice of duty. I utilized introspection, challenging my state of nature and how my self-centered designs constituted a compromised navigation system, leading me to dead-end after dead-end. They led me down a very dark path in life, away from the light of my essence. Simply put, those self-centered designs were my character flaws. My greatest faults in life, at least up until that point, were to be conscious of none. I had no clue who I was. Demanding an answer, I needed to question my self-centered designs. Funny thing; solitude became fertile soil for self-discovery.

My journey toward liberation was spawned when taking my first step toward obtaining a college education. During my first semester in college, I read an excerpt from "The Tao of Success", by Derek Lin. He described the transformative power of alchemy, in that change is a central characteristic of the mind; understanding how to utilize baser instincts and turning them into noble ideals. Destructive impulses into something constructive. He offered a story about an old man who always got angry when he was young. The old man recognized that his anger could be destructive to himself and others, so decided to run when he got angry. This fuel to exercise reaped healthy benefits, and a clarity of mind as he redirected his energy to the physical task. The steps necessary to conduct negative to positive is the following:

(1) Take a step back mentally so you can evaluate the negative feeling(s) objectively.
(2) Think about your purpose in life.
(3) Put the negative feeling next to your purpose, and weigh them out.

Using this method brought me some clarity to my unexamined life. I began to redirect my negative energy and put it into my quest for higher learning.

When I felt I had no answers to my day-to-day problems, I sought refuge in my college materials, and related resources. Information I read to help me with my quest led me down the most unlikeliest path: altruism. I found healing powers when given an opportunity to help others. I found purpose in uplifting others. But most of all, I found freedom while helping those in need. No journey is easy, otherwise everyone would be accomplished without putting in much effort, patience, or sacrifice. The greater the effort, the greater the reward.

I had dealth with problems in each of my semesters while in college. They ranged from not having the ability to purchase necessary materials; receiving an 'F' grade in a course I wasn't enrolled in; having an incompetent proctor take away my e-reader, with my college books downloaded on it, because of his error (which is much worse in prison, where there is no recourse, than it would be on the streets); dropping courses because my textbooks were "Returned to Sender" because R&R (Receiving and Release) at my institution thought my books were contraband; to having purposely dropped one course only to have my college's administration mistakenly drop me from other courses as well. My college journey has been difficult, and less than ideal.

At times I've wondered if I should continue pursuing my degree when it seemed like an uphill battle at every turn. I've thought, "it shouldn't be this difficult". Then, I think about my father who had traveled so far from home, enduring unthinkable struggles both physical and mental in order to capitalize on an opportunity. I think about that opportunity that stands before me to get a free college education while in prison, after shirking my role in society and rebelling against what was expected of me: to obey the law and not cause fear of violent death to citizens. In order to demonstrate true remorse, which is a change of behavior, I must capitalize on all opportunities set before me to be redeemed. I must give whatever effort is necessary. The greater the effort, the greater the reward.

For my collegiate efforts, I have garnered three degrees:

(1) Associate in Arts in Social and Behavioral Sciences.
(2) Associate in Arts in American Studies.
(3) Associate in Arts in Arts and Humanities.

These parchments illustrating my awards are fulfilling. No piece of paper, however, will ever make me soar higher than the wisdom I've gained on this journey. I've become more self-aware, patient, goal-oriented, selfless, kind determined, humble, disciplined, and liberated.

In 'The Republic', Plato's Cave Allegory, he depicts a group of people in shackles. Conditions of their confinement allowed only the shadows dancing on the cave's walls to be their reality. Unbeknownst to the prisoners, there were people on the other side, outside of their view, moving about in front of a fire causing their silhouettes to be the projections onto the cave's walls. Those shadows were all the prisoners knew to be real; their truth. We owe it to ourselves to discover our own personal truths and become free. It is a journey. But the journey to freedom is easiest by taking the first step.

Jose Duarte
AI-5098

JAMES WILSON

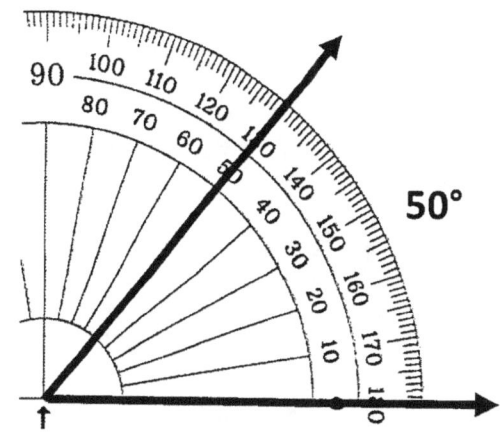

BE INSPIRED

"I am a citizen of the world."
- Diodenes, Greek Philosopher

Tore from the Flag by Men of the Cloth

Take this journey with me. The experiences and situations I will discuss here happened around me, and to me. Some even came as a result of me. But, they are not me. To make this all about me would be to limit the scope of what I am trying to share with every reader. This is about all of us.

No matter how distant, detached, or exculpable any of us believe we are to the events and circumstances that occur, from our household to the world at large, we all share (by omission or commission) some liability for the things that happen around us. This lesson was brought home by the contrast between the responsibilities taken on by climate activist Greta Thunberg (a private citizen, and teenager), and the shirking of all responsibility by former President Donald Trump. Even (and especially) of problems he created himself, or ones he could have controlled from "the most powerful office in the world"! Knowledge is power, so whether you're in the highest office in the land, or are a private citizen with the capacity for awareness, you bear some responsibility for the conditions on this planet.

I am in prison, like millions of other men, women, and young people in the "Free World". There are very few other places in the world (aside from poor communities of color, and third world countries) where you so starkly see the cumulative effect of the lack of responsibility taken by governments, elected officials, private citizens, and "the system" (which is ran by people, not autonomously). The weight of our collective failures seem always to come crashing down, and reveal themselves the most, amongst the most poor and least (economically and politically) powerful. The greatest evidence is to be found in these places: in poor communities, third world countries, and yes... prisons. Read the following article written by the former Secretary of the California Department of Corrections and Rehabilitation:

Now is the Time to Not be Silent
By Secretary Ralph Diaz
June 12, 2020

Since mid-March, CDCR and the nation have been nothing like 'normal programming', and I ask myself: "Will we ever return to normal?" Rather than attempt to find ways to make the normal we are all familiar with fit into the new realities, I have to be honest: I am looking forward to not going back to normal program. This pandemic, followed by the national attention on law enforcement reform, have thrust us into the perfect moment to recreate this great agency once again. This is not the time for yearning for the good old days - and need I remind you, those days were only 90 days ago. If we do not put thought into action and start this recrafting of CDCR for the better, others will.

What we have learned about COVID-19 is it spreads swiftly, and without much notice until someone starts showing signs of symptoms. As a system we are making changes and creating strategies on how to battle the spread. I cannot help but find parallels with COVID and its spread and impacts, to the right scrutiny the law enforcement community is receiving from the public we are hired to serve. We in CDCR are not immune from this scrutiny, nor should we be.

A virus grows in silence, but it's effects are as destructive as racism, injustice, marginalization, and indifference. In my nearly 30 years in this great organization of CDCR I have sadly seen them all. As the Secretary of this great Agency, I have the responsibility to stand and use my voice and position to say now is the time to not be silent. I have a limited time in this position, and if I waste it playing it safe by remaining silent I allow the virus of hate to exist and spread. Now is the time to speak truth from the place that makes us who we truly are: from the heart.

I know when a vaccine is created we will be relieved, looking to return to normal program and work and home. I am not looking forward to returning to normal program if that means we are not ready to acknowledge that we need to change how we treat everyone in our system and how we treat eachother. We have the greatest opportunity to be the example of change.

This pandemic has brought to light the true capability of our Agency to come together not only across multiple professional disciplines, but across designations of staff, incarcerated persons, family members, activists, and legislators - to work together to protect the people in our care and hold one another accountable. We have tragically lost two staff members and 15 incarcerated people to this disease, and I pray those numbers do not increase. As my heart breaks for those we have lost, I am also inspired by the bravery, dedication, and innovative spirit I see every day as the exceptional employees of this Department give their all under unprecedented challenges, and under intense scrutiny, to battle this disease.

We will come through this pandemic as a better agency. I am just as confident that with the right courage and reflection, we will come through our unrest as a better nation. The tragic death of George Floyd has sparked outrage and cries for reform, but it is so important to remember that George Floyd's death is not the first injustice marginalized people have experienced in this world.

Please do not let my words be the only ones you read on this subject. I challenge every person who reads this to go outside their comfort zone, do your own research, and engage in conversations with people you may not normally interact with. Speak to someone who looks different from you, or who grew up in different circumstances.

I challenge you to treat all around you with respect and understanding, regardless of their status, skin color, or background.

By the time someone is sentenced to state prison, in the vast majority of instances, they have been failed by system after system along the way. Do not let CDCR be another destination of failure. Compassion and communication do not mean sacrificing security - in fact, by acting with professionalism and respect with our colleagues and those we serve, we build trust, and that trust results in safer prisons and communities.

Martin Luther King Jr. said: "I have decided to stick with love. Hate is to great a burden to bear." The only vaccine for racism, injustice, marginalization, and indifference is love. In the darkest of places in our system, the only light that shines through is love. I love this calling and deliver this message to all of you in love.

With gratitude and respect,

Ralph M. Diaz
Secretary, CDCR
https://www.cdcr.ca.gov/insidecdcr/2020/06/12/now-is-the-time-to-not-be-silent/

We can no longer be silent about the viruses of racism, hate, injustice, marginalization, and indifference! The COVID pandemic revealed that to us. COVID (the full weight of it) fell heaviest upon the most vulnerable in every society. Prior to COVID every system was silmilarly failing us: the educational, political, and economic systems, as well as our religious, insurance, and medical institutions; not to mention the juvenile and adult criminal justice systems (police brutality and mass incarceration). As was said by one who experienced both prison and political power, former South African President Nelson Mandela:

> "It is said that no one
> truly knows a nation until
> one has been inside its
> jails. A nation should
> not be judge by how
> it treats its highest
> citizens, but its lowest ones."

I think it was also the late Mandela who said: "Poverty is man-made. So it can be un-made by man." There are problems created by man that only man can solve. Including the man-made systems we live under.

There is a reason we have "high" and "low" citizens, and it's not all about meritocracy, or people failing for lack of agency (remember the college admission scandals, the poll tax, and the real benefitiaries of the New Deal, welfare, and affirmative action). This list could also include the emancipation proclamation and it's correlatives (the 13th Amendment, Jim Crowism, tough-on-crime laws, etc.). Systems such as these can be designed to lift, or lower, people depending upon their race, position, economic status, gender, or other demographics.

Without exempting poor people of some of the responsibility for allowing their conditions to persist, we should understand that these conditions weren't created in a vacuum. One must educate oneself to the systemic mechanisms that have echoed down through history that have upheld, and allowed the persistence of, such conditions to appreciate their complexities in full. Things didn't just happen. Powerful people throughout history made, and are making, things happen. Since we already know that (in America, and much of the rest of the Western World) wealth is synonomous with power, we have a responsibility in this government "of, for, and by the people" to attain some of this power for ourselves, right? "Power tends to concede nothing without a demand," as Frederick Douglass said, so we must demand equity and justice.

The Declaration of Independence gives the citizens the right to change their government if it isn't working for them. The reasons it hasn't changed are legion, but at the top of the list is that the government and economy (capitalism) does work for lots of people. Especially those people with wealth and capital! Make no mistake about it. Our Democracy began with it's roots in the ideas of monarchy and oligarchy: the rule by the few over the many.

Don't you think it's time for a change? How do we make the majority rule a true reality? How do we hold our representatives accountable? The "powers to the people" (or the social contract): freedom of speech, the right to protest, seek redress, the legal right to vote, equal protection under the law, benefits of services for taxes and citizenship, etc., are not to be taken for granted. As Ronald Reagan stated (and I paraphrase here): "Our freedoms can be lost in a single generation." The generations following the Voting and Civil Rights acts of 1964-65 are a good example of this. Many precious freedoms have been curtailed. This has been a pattern, reminding us that freedom isn't free.

A study of what happened between the issuance of the Emancipation Proclamation (1863) and the period known as Reconstruction (1867-1891) reveal this very thing. Extraordinary agency was shown on behalf of freed slaves with rightful assistance from their government and other agencies, only to have the progress completely collapse by the rise of the KKK, government collusion, and failed political will. Within a generation the freed men, and women, had lost all of their so-called freedoms. Freedoms they have yet to fully enjoy even today (2021), over a hundred years later!

It took people, and systems, to bring people low. People that called themselves the highest, or white supremacists. I am a descendant of those slaves that won, then lost, so much in that period, and so I carry much of their legacy: the pain, trials, and wounds on one end, and the hopes, dreams, and aspirations on the other. Freedom is a constant struggle, as Angela Davis teaches, and each generation has to do it's part. I grew up in 'the hood' in third world-like conditions. My mother was a single parent, teaching me what domestic failure looks like. Like me, most of my childhood friends had no father in their homes. With only an eighth-grade education, my mother raised seven children while living on welfare in a drug and gang infested housing project called "Kings Manor". We were ostensibly the 'peasants' on 'the Kings' plot of land, but we fought over it like we were it's noble class!

What follows is 'an evidence of one'. Although my own story is just one among many that can attest similarly:

Our gangs gave us a vehicle to express our pain and anger ("Riots are the voice of the unheard!"), and we spent most of our tenure burning down our own community and hurting our own kind. I would later learn that this was a symptom of a psychological disease. A legacy of slavery termed, 'self-hatred'. It was, according to Malcolm X, America's greatest crime: teaching black people how to hate each other.

We were made in America, and like the slaves I took on the name of my abuser. I was known in the streets as 'Lil' Sleprock', the nickname of ill fortune, or bad luck. I became a carrier of pain and personal self-hatred, and I went about making sure everyone heard, and felt, my pain. I made a reputation throughout Pasadena, California for hurting other poor and powerless people. Sadly, other hurt kids (looking for recognition) began looking up to me, just like we were taught in school, movies, and music to admire "bad" people. People like Alexander the Great, Constantine, and many of our country's fore-fathers (among others). People who murdered, raped, enslaved and/or pillaged entire countries became our heroes. The schools themselves did not speak to my pain. Neither did the religious institutions. To a certain extent, by not mining the role models they gave us, these institutions (on balance) gave us examples that aided the perpetuation of our self-hatred, and misery. They had all betrayed the poor for money from 'the King' (the state) to keep their doors open and their incomes flowing. All we got in return was more Jesus and jails.

I found myself in and out of the system: juvenile halls, camps, and California Youth Authority (CYA) from ages thirteen to twenty-one. I "graduated" to the adult criminal justice system less than forty days after exiting the juvenile system. I went to prison for murder at twenty-one.

While in the juvenile system I discovered not education or rehabilitation, but every artifice needed to become a more sophisticated criminal. This school-to-prison pipeline, and the radicalization of gangs, is happening all across America. We had older inmates to teach us the ropes, and staff who supplied us with pornography, cigarrettes, liquor, and weed. They even gave us weekend "fight nights" to settle our personal feuds, or gang beefs. We had been given such licence by people who were paid with taxpayers money to protect and serve us. There was a communal library mostly full of street novels by Donald Goines, and Bibles for us to read. Many of us aspired to be better gangsters, pimps, or preachers: sharp with our hands, our tongues, or both! We would exercise all of this learning (filled with unhealed pain and anger) on members of our own communities.

"The greatest weapon of the oppressor," Steven Biko said, "is the minds of the oppressed." We had a mindset that forever worked against our own survival and progress. Our goal was to collectivize our learning for profit and personal power, like modern-day sellouts.

After the 1992 L.A. riots, many of the black kids in CYA got turned on to black history and literature. This learning process converted many young men to Islam, and pro-blackness. It was the first time I witnessed something begin to loosen the chains of the gang mentality, and black-on-black violence in my community. There was talk of a "peace treaty" between Crips and Bloods following the riots, and for a short period in CYA gang violence declined as it had in the street and throughout Los Angeles County. The message was: "Love your own, and do something for yourself." There was the idea of rebuilding the black community, policing our own neighborhoods, ending black-on-black crime, and creating black owned businesses. A new form of black Reconstruction; born out of the teachings of Marcus Garvey and the Honorable Elijah Muhammad.

Sometime in 1993, I got the opportunity to read the autobiography of Malcolm-X. I was seventeen years old and on my second CYA term, with a head full of Donald Goines books, Bible verses, and bitterness. I had no knowledge of the fact that most of what I was reading in the Bible was part of black history, so about a year later I converted to Sunni Islam. For a period I belonged to the Ansar-El-Muhammads, and later fell in with the Nation of Islam (NOI) under the leadership of Minister Louis Farrakhan. The Malcolm-X book and the Holy Quran helped me put black history and religious history into a rational perspective. These tools provided me with some causative reality of why the world in general, and black people in particular, were in their current predicament.

Prior to reading the autobiography of Malcolm-X, I thought everyone was a Christian, and that our place in the world was "normal". I did not see religion, and human history, as a continuum. That at one time Judaism was a dominant religion in the old world (prior to Christianity), and Africans were the first civilization builders.

I had no knowledge of Islam. I always thought that the black guys selling bean pies and news papers in the neighborhood were Jehovahs Witnesses, not members of NOI. We stayed away from them. In the past, when I had read my Bible, I had 'naturally' assumed that all the characters and lands were white, and white owned. Just like I saw in school, church, and the movies. I had no other references for assessing other religions, and how they relate to

---

*John Potash in "FBI Wars Against Tupac and Other Black Leaders" presents evidence from actual police sources stating that some cops broke up the peace treaty.
*See, African Origin of Civilization, by Cheik Anta Diop.

black history. My mind was a repository for pain and fables.

I came into contact with great literature and informed older youth wards in CYA, who tried to shake gang banging and self-hatred out of me. By nineteen years old, and ready for my second parole, I left CYA "talking black". This was 1994. I was giving myself a shot at freedom.

My mother, recently 'reborn' and on fire for Jesus, couldn't take my new diet (no pork) and praying to some heathen "God" named Allah. We were having domestic "religious wars", which forced me out of her home and onto the streets once again with only my new theoretical basis for living. It wasn't long before I hooked up with the homies, and the madness of the streets.

Thinking back, my mother demonstrated less fury over my joining the neighborhood gang at thirteen than when learning I had converted to Islam. I fell back on my 'practical', but destructive, life-style. Before that, I had stopped smoking and using drugs. I stayed in the house praying and reading, and wasn't 'hanging out'. Even my homies were shocked, but impressed as well. I thought that I was slowly freeing myself. Unfortunately, I was also back in the streets with a vengeance, and feeling rejected and dispossessed.

I started oppressing my own kind again. In retrospect, some of my homies were disappointed, except for those who relied upon my gangsterism. An extension of our collective self-hatred, and crimes against poor and powerless people. We had become our own enemies. The same phase the Brazilian author of the "Pedagogy of the Oppressed", as well as Frantz Fanon, wrote about that occurred with recently freed oppressed people in Algeria and Brazil. After a third CYA violation, and so-called "freedom" (for forty days), I found myself on my way to prison at twenty-one years old (1996). Heading up the river on the 'slave ship' (prison bus) towards the modern-day 'plantation' (as we called it).

I had seen so many juvenile "converts" relapse back into crime, black-on-black violence, and recidivism. We were back in the 'field': hooking, jabbing, and stabbing one another. The spell was as yet un-broken, and with our new-found "education" and criminal sophistication we were favored to rise to leadership positions within the gang, and the system (like the overseers before us). We fell against eachother like a house divided. We had broken our agreements with God and men - covenant and peace treaty. Black Reconstruction was to be delayed once again.

We seemed to be fighting harder for re-enslavement than our ancestors had for our collective freedom. Martin Luther King Jr., other Civil Rights leaders, and Black Liberation veterans were turning in their graves. We had

---

* Paulo Freire, the Brazilian educator, wrote "Pedagogy of the Oppressed."
Frantz Fanon, the Algerian revolutionary, wrote "Black Skin, White Mask."

spit upon our inheritance of freedom and love, and chose other forms of slavery and hatred instead. We would pay a heavy price for our betrayal. For me, it would take another decade, degrees of suffering, additional parole violations, and another black-on-black homicide when I was thirty years old for a new learning experience to take shape in my life.

In the NOI we learned that knowledge comes in steps, stages, and degrees. Like the sunlight that is ever-present, but visits different regions around the globe in separate time zones, there are sleep-to-wake cycles in the growing process. In 2005 I was back in L.A. County Jail fighting a capital murder case, facing the death penalty yet experiencing a rebirth. Something inside me (a voice? some remaining will-power? destiny?) would not permit me to lay down and "die" (both figuratively and literally). I had to desire life as a prerequisite to any form of freedom.

I was tossed into a dungeon (a place called 'High Power') with serious offenders like myself, and prison gang leaders: Mexican Mafia, Black Guerilla Family, and Arian Brotherhood members. There were also "drop outs", and gang members formed from that class of inmate as well. This was a new playing field where I saw first-hand the disintegration of loyalty, leadership, and structures.

Luckily, we were all single-celled, which provided me great time and space for reflection, introspection, and reading. I was also able to "study" the leadership style, structure, and prison gang philosophy of other races. Little did I know at the time that I'd be in the county jail for close to a decade. With all this time I found myself revisiting much of my own personal experiences, as well as educating myself about world history and world religions. It became apparent to me that many of our brown and white brothers were victims of the same system as black people. We are all products of the "American Experiment", and were all searching for meaning, purpose, and power. Just on a smaller stage (the hood and prison).

I found out that many of these men were brilliant. They could articulate like professors. Some even had college degrees, owned businesses, and dreamed of a life beyond gangs and crime. This is where I first learned to distinguish "bad acts" from "bad people". We were all living out self-fulfilled prophecies from decades of learned behavior. This was behavior we could unlearn, however, if we chose too. We had to take responsibility for our recovery, and redemption.

It was at this time that I was given books about the F.B.I.'s counter-intelligence program (COINTEL-PRO), where I learned how our own government had deliberately infiltrated, divided, and destroyed labor movements, anti-war

---

*Read my other book "Evidence of Long, lost Letters" for insight about the rampant and wreckless use of informants.

organizations, and the American Indian, Civil Rights, and Black Liberation movements. Our own government went after white, black, brown, red, and yellow! Basically, anyone who opposed the governments agenda. They had turned the east and west coast Black Panthers against each other. A rift that resulted in bloodshed, the destruction of the BPP, and dozens of false imprisonments. I read what the U.S. government had done to Nelson Mandela, Henry David Thoreau, Leonald Peltier, Geronimo Pratt, Malcolm X, Martin Luther King Jr., Fred Hampton, and countless more of it's own citizens, with taxpayers money.

Although I was guilty as hell for killing another black man, I found out through discovery items provided by the government that cops on my case (and in other cases) had several young, unregistered, and unpaid informants spying on members of the black community. These informants were allowed to violate their parole and probation; even to commit crimes, with impunity. We were all pawns in a game that was far bigger than us. Sitting me down in the worst conditions, and situation, raised my consciousness many degrees. I was beginning to piece together the bigger picture. Each year new scales fell from my eyes, allowing more light to come through. But, light comes by degrees.

In 2007, after two years in the jail, I met my spiritual mentor and friend, Chaplain Nagy. Nagy was a white man, and a Buddhist master. Through years of visits and teachings he dusted my mind and heart of anger, bitterness, and resentments. "Be aware of the man with the learning from just one book," Nagy taught me. Nagy had served in the Korean War as a para-trooper. He also worked in prisons, mental hospitals for the criminally insane, and had travelled to over 30 countries in his lifetime. The man brought a lot to the table, and I had the good fortune to have more than seven years in the jail to learn from him before going off to prison.

This man wanted to expand my horizons. Every week he found his way into the jail to liberate me. One day, standing at my cell, looking at me through steel bars, Nagy said: "James, I know why you're here. But, I am not here to condemn you." He went on to say that I had a great mind and a life ahead of me, even if I landed on death row. Nagy had committed himself to my good future, even unto death! He taught me how, after the Buddha gained enlightenment and freedom from suffering, he delayed his transition to Nirvana in order to save (free) others here on Earth. He spent fifty plus years seeking to do so. It was the duty of a Bodhisatva (one who delays transition) to help others.

Nagy explained to me that all true leaders teach freedom. He taught me that Moses, Jesus, Buddha, Confucius, and Muhammad were all freedom fighters. They came to free men from political, economic, and social bondage. Which, he explained, came from bad ideas. He would always quote Voltaire (the enlightenment philosopher), saying, "very few people escape the idea of their times." He taught me how Muhammad said, "false ideas are the worst form of oppression." Therefore, every era had it's "slaves"; mental slaves. This is why every culture also produces it's liberators. A necessity for any rational and equitable society; to free people from the bad ideas of their times.

Nagy told me many times: "James, you are a Bhodisatva, and your mission is to free others from the bad ideas of gangs and violence." His message resonated with alot of what I had learned in my NOI lessons. I could relate.

In 2009, at age thirty-four, I started breaking away from gang ideology. First, by dropping my gang name (Sleprock II) and only responding to my Arabic name: Ansar. Ansar means helper. This was the name given to me in 1994 when I became a Muslim. The Bay Area rapper Askari X (Ricky Murdock) blessed me with this title while we were neighbors in CYA, but I had to grow still, by degrees, into the "function" of a helper.

We were taught in our NOI lessons that "the negro must be raised from a horizontal state of death to a living perpendicular". Basically, in stages; by degrees. We were taught that "negro" meant mental/spiritual death, and true knowledge, learned over time, would resurrect us.

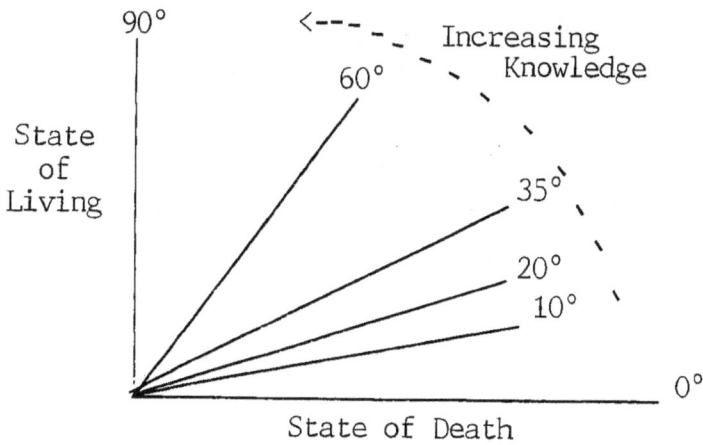

I remember when I was in prison in my 20's and a man told me: "just because the Bible says that light shined out of darkness doesn't mean it happened in an instant." It is only logical to believe that the darkness did resist, he concluded. This was evidenced in my personal study of the Quran where all religious books (the Torah, the Gospel, and the Quran itself) are called "lights".

They all appeared in times of mass spiritual and moral darkness. It is why Muslims pray five times a day, at different stages of the light, praying more frequently as day-light declines. Later I discovered that in every culture a wise person was styled as the sun or the moon - a light bearer. Light, consciousness, and change come by degrees; gradually.

There is much meaning in a name, as I shared with you about Sleprock. In the Jewish culture it is taught that three things can change a person's destiny. They are: (1) Sincere prayers; (2) Charity; and (3) a change of name. Muslims are taught not to have "nicknames" after choosing faith. Names have power. Words have power. A bad name can obscure vision (faith) and delay destiny!

Prior to my arrest, my mother came into the parking stall of her apartment complex where I was holding a small meeting with some gang members. She would often tell me and my other brothers that we were leaders, and could lead men to school, church, or to anything positive. "People", she said, "followed us for our leadership, not just because it was negative." This day though, she stood stone-faced with her arms crossed, in front of my homies, staring at me only hours after my release from a parole violation and said: "James, you are a leader. God wants you. And if you don't walk away from that gang stuff, God is gonna tear you away from it."

I didn't walk away. I finished the meeting and we set off into the night to commit more crimes. I was back in custody not long afterwards, and within weeks my nephew, "Milk Man", was killed. A few weeks after that my brother, Johnathen, was murdered. Obviously, not everyone would make it to the end game, even the best and brightest.

I paroled again in 2005 after serving eleven months for a parole violation, but I wasn't yet ready for freedom and would be jailed again within months. This time I did try to do right, even with a heavy heart set on revenge. I had gotten a job, participated in 'Stop the Violence', and police killing protests. Unfortunately, the streets were still calling after me, and so were my rivals.

The events leading up to my 2005 capital murder case put me in a position where I fell out with the gangs so badly that I could never return to it's ranks. I was literally, as my mom predicted, tore from the flag (the gang). The 'universe' knew that I would not walk away of my own volition. The chains had to be forcefully broken in order for me to take a free step, and reach a new degree of growth and progress. I was thirty years old now, and the light

---

*Read my other book "Evidence of Long, Lost Letters" to learn more about the cause of my fall-out with my former gang.

and lessons were finally gonna have their way with me. After all, I was to spend almost the next ten years in county jail. Thankfully, I was spared a death sentence and got a new lease on life.

Now, I opened this chapter saying that this was not "all about me", and I've tried to spread the cream over the entire cake from the systemic, to the personal, to help you to place yourself in my shoes. Maybe if you allow yourself to experience the effects from my perspective, you won't want anything to do with all the negative causes! Every one should permit themselves a moment to reflect on periods in their lives when enlightenment (through experience or mentors) tried to pierce the veil of their ignorance, or conditioning. At every stage of our growth someone, or some-thing, appears that allows us to glimpse, or experience, new windows of opportunity. Street knowledge, or street smarts, can only take you so far. It usually only takes you down a dead end road.

When I was young, I learned that drugs were put into black and brown communities to destroy people of color. At that age though, it really didn't move me to reconsider my role in all this tragedy; even though I personally saw how it ravished our communities, claiming the lives of many of my friends and family. Even as I sold drugs, I had a personal dislike for using them, and some guilt for selling them at an early age. So, I began finding new ways to make money. I was twenty-one (twenty-five years ago!) when, as a full fledged gang member, I gave up smoking weed and drinking alcohol. Something pulled me away from them early in life. This has allowed me to have good health, a great attention span, and a robust memory in my forties. I am benefiting today from decisions made decades ago. Everything, as I look back, happened for a reason in my life.

Some growth processes can only occur over large spans of time. The hands on life's clock swing wide. I sat on the stoop at twelve and thirteen years old listening to my older homies who came out of juvenile camps, CYA, and prison. Bending my ear to the lessons about the hood, the "enemy", the cops, and surviving inside the system. I knew I was headed for the game, so why not learn from the coaches and the best players (for that level of the game)? I would even listen to O.G.'s from the opposite side of the track. This open-minded learning approach would help me in my latter years.

We learned in the NOI, despite it's view of white people, that:

1. Many white people would assist in the liberation of black people;
2. Many white people in secret societies professed Islam;

3. The founder of the NOI, Master Fard Muhammad, was half-white.

The Honorable Elijah Muhammad once told Farrakhan: "Don't throw trash in a well I seek to take a drink from," allegorically telling Farrakhan to not teach in a way that destroys opportunities to reach out to white people. In the same vein he stated that, "if you hate white people, then you won't learn from them", professing that one should be willing to take truth wherever it comes from by saying, "if you are used to eating food off of a gold platter and you are hungry and someone offers you food on a silver platter, then, eat it."

In NOI we were taught that we would have friendships in <u>all</u> walks of life. There's even a part of the lessons where it says: "a black man can turn devil overnight." Minister Farrakhan teaches that anyone with moral knowledge that won't make moral corrections is a devil. I've known a lot of black devils. I was one of them.

When I met Nagy, a white man, in the Los Angeles County jail, I was hungry - starving actually - and he came in with all kinds of delicious food for thought! He fed my mind, and my soul, without concerns about my race, my crimes, or my religious beliefs. He'd say: "I heard Farrakhan before. Boy, he can sure preach a good sermon! Get them folks all fired up over whitey." Then, he'd burst out laughing. Nagy really loved a good black preacher. He said that no one ever turned preaching into an art form quite like the black church. He admired T.D. Jakes and Malcolm X. Nagy told me (in so many ways) that black lives, and black leadership, mattered.

In the beginning of our relationship he only wanted to give me books I requested. Seeing the pattern he'd say: "What black person do you wanna read about now?" After a few years, I flipped it on him and said: "give me some books about you crazy white people!" He laughed all over that, but true to his word, he did.

He brought me dozens of books on European and early American history. I know it made him proud to pump me full of white history! Not to mention what he shared on world history, and religions. He'd always tell me (he repeated himself a lot): "James, us Irish people had it just as rough as black people, once upon a time, in America. My people arrived here on ships, too." His ancestors arrived here during the Potato Famine in Ireland in the 1800's.

Nagy shared with me his own spiritual evolution. His late father, he told me, had been a Christian and a racist. Nagy himself had been a Catholic, a Quaker, and then a Buddhist. His wife, Gale, was Jewish. Then, one day in

2009, he came onto the tier and to my cell and asked: "how would you like to meet one of my Jewish friends? I call him a 'Jew-Bu'."

He told me his friend's name was Brian, and he taught inner-city school aged kids. He was a teacher of some sort. I knew from past studies that Rabbi meant teacher (or master) in Hebrew, 'nourisher unto perfection' in Arabic, and 'Lord' in English. I knew my education was on an increasingly forward trajectory.

After meeting him, I began receiving small cards with brief inspiring messages inside them from "Rabbi Brian". It turned out that Rabbi Brian taught mathematics at a junior high school, and was also the founder of "Religion-Outside-the-Box". He even wrote a newsletter, full of wisdom, forty weeks out of a year called 'the 77% weekly'. He was not a traditional Rabbi, but a master teacher of the treasure of world religions. Seven is the number of God and perfection. We became pen-pals, and then great friends; family even. This relationship also spread to his wife, Jane (a Catholic), and their two kids - Anne and Emmett.

Six years into our friendship, in 2015, Rabbi Brian was terminated from his teaching position for permitting me, a prisoner, to write and mentor his students. Obviously, I was hurt by this, and blamed myself for it all. The Rabbi, in his great wisdom, told me: "James, it is no fault of yours. I work at a Christian school that teaches people to look after prisoners. The fault is their own." I knew from that day forward that we were true friends.

Unfortunately, Nagy transitioned in 2016 to Nirvana at 80+ years old, having "saved" me at one stage, then passing me off to Rabbi Brian to complete the work. Nagy liked to say: "one candle can light a thousand." Starting with Nagy, Rabbi Brian and his wife Jane, I now have friends (all of them white!) all over the United States and other countries. They are my greatest friends, and helpers. I call them 'light-bearers'. Everybody needs light in a dark place (prison).

During all the racial unrest following George Floyds killing, Rabbi Brian led protests in Portland (Oregon), taught on anti-racism, and wrote articles to his readership on why Jewish people should support the Black Lives Matter movement. He even supports a small black Jewish community in Africa. I knew these good people came into my life to help me bring it full circle.

Rabbi Brian has nurtured me - mind and spirit - and built a family of support around me. Especially Alex Taylor and Robin Shanker, my other long time Jewish friends, as well as many others unnamed here. They have all fought on my behalf against a racist, and reactionary, prison system (High Desert State Prison) that militates against rehabilitation (in a so called "rehabilitation center" - paid for with tax payers money!). Thankfully, for support, loyalty to truth, freedom, and progress, I have (despite all the systemic opposition) co-founded five self-help groups in this prison alone. This, and my new disposition, has allowed me to help many men along on their own paths of transformation. I have been finally paying it forward. Becoming a true helper!

    I know that I am not truly free until we are all free. However, everything comes in steps, stages, and degrees. As the Chinese say: "the journey of a million miles begins with the first step."

    Looking back, one of the greatest affirmations of my spiritual and intellectual progress came 2014, just prior to a settlement being reached in my case. My mother (Connie) came to visit me in L.A. County jail, and she said: "James, I am your mother. I know my children. I can tell you have truly changed. I can hear it in your voice. I don't know what it is, Allah or whatever, but I see it." This time, she spoke Allah's name without derision or disrespect. Times had definately changed!

By: James Wilson

ADRIAN WOODARD

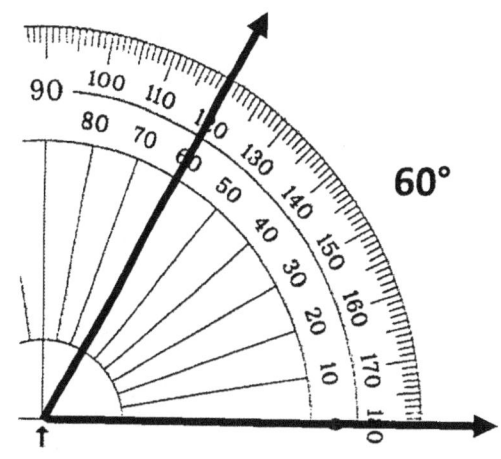

LEADERS ARE READERS

"A people without the knowledge of their past history,
origin, and culture is like a tree without roots."

- Marcus Garvey

My Two Roads Travelled

Let me start with some introductions. In the early 1960's, my grandmother (Altha Mae Evans), her sister (Annie Mae Evans), and their brother (Frank Evans) moved from East Texas to a small farm community in El Nido, California; located a few miles outside of Merced, in Central California. My mother (Barbara Lorraine Calhoun) was her first born and had three siblings: a brother (Glenn Greene), and two sisters (Felicia Greene and Cynthia Gordon. Barbara (my mother) had four children: Althena Woodard-Hendricks, Adrian Woodard Sr. (myself), Randall Slaton, and Tremaine Slaton. Our family was tight nit, and would live in the same home in El Nido until the late 1970's.

While I was still in El Nido, I can remember chasing chickens, playing with pigs, and trying to run down jack rabbits. The only time I can remember getting into any trouble there was when my cousin, Sterling Hollis (now deceased), and myself swam in an irrigation ditch. My great aunt (Annie Mae) caught us and told us to rinse off in one of the outside showers. While rinsing off, she came into the shower and whooped us with a switch. Otherwise, all of my early childhood memories were pleasant and filled with good times. My Great Uncle Frank had his children there with us too; as did Cynthia. Those were the good-ol'-days.

Eventually, Altha Mae decided that she wanted to complete her education. After she graduated from college, she relocated to Stockton, California with my Aunt Cynthia. Never one to settle, my grandmother moved again to Ione, California, becoming a teacher in one of the Youth Authority prisons (C.Y.A.) - Preston School of Industry. As fortune would have it, my mother decided to pitch her own tent in Stockton, and that is where my formative years took place. I would grow of age in Stockton. Unfortunately, things began to change for my mother once we moved there.

There were numerous boyfriends, and an increase in alcohol consumption. The home became a battleground between my mother, and her male acquaintances. This brought the police to our house on a regular basis for domestic violence calls. Even though I was young, I tried to prevent my mother from being abused. While I couldn't stop the violence, I did develop tactics to keep it at a minimum. When my Uncle (Glenn Greene) moved to Stockton after discharging from the military, things changed again.

I was instructed to contact him if ever there was a problem. On a few occasions this worked, and the beatings would stop for a while. Then, there were times I was unable to contact him, and was forced to watch the abuse that my mother suffered. I can remember how helpless I felt. These men seemed like monsters to me. I swore that I'd get even when I got bigger. I knew that this would take too long, however.

My equalizer came when I joined a gang. A place where violence was always an option to deal with any situation. My desire to stop men from abusing my mother would come at a great cost. Not to the men who perpetrated the violence upon my mother, but to countless others. This was due to my becoming the monster I despised.

I had served time in California's Youth Authority, and had earned a solid reputation in my neighborhood. This afforded me the "leadership", and influence, to get my homies to follow me. To do as I told them; including to hurt people. I wanted to exact revenge on those men who had beaten my mother for years. To my surprise though, drugs and alcohol had turned these so-called 'monsters' (including the father of my brother Randall), into harmless wimps. They were not even worth the time, and energy, I had mustered for them.

While I succeeded in seeing to it that my mother was never beaten up again, I became the person who would beat and victimize others. This included the people close to me. Of course, I made every excuse, and/or justification, for my atrocious behavior; but the fact remained that I had become the very person I despised. My criminality and drug use eventually escalated to the point where my thinking, and belief system, was so warped that I attempted to kill a police officer; Officer Kevin Bertalotto.

Even in my darkest moment I was not able to see who, or what, I had become. My family became memories to me. I abandoned my two children, Adrienne Woodard and Adrian Woodard Jr. I came to prison and entrenched myself in prison politics, and advancing the illegitimate authority of the gang. I had done so well at building my identity around these things. Or so I thought!

> "Self-knowledge is the basis of true knowledge."
> - Kemetic Proverb

After spending 14 years displaying self-destructive behavior in prison, I began to become disillusioned with the life that I was living. In 2008-09 I was in CSP-Corcoran's ad-seg (the hole) when I discovered the need to cultivate my spirit. I didn't know what I was looking for, but I knew I had to find it. Before I was transferred from Kern Valley State Prison to Corcoran in 2008 (pre ad-seg experience), I had an opportunity to learn about an ancient African spirituality: (Kemetic) Nterianism. Unfortunately, I was transferred before I could really study or learn anything. In 2009 I was released back into Corcoran's general population determined to change myself. I became a vegan, and meditated regularly. One day, While I was in the chow hall explaining to one of my homeboys what I'd learned about Nterianism, another man at an adjacent table introduced himself to me as 'Imakhu', and informed me that he was a 'Nterian' and could supply me with materials to learn from if I so desired.

    I engulfed myself into the Kemetic spirituality known as Nterianism. I studied and learned that there was a way for me to cultivate my spirit that was not at odds with what I already believed to be absolute truth. I became an 'Aspirant', and as my thinking changed I began to have conflicts with my homeboys. I could no longer follow my former morality blindly. I was now aware that many of my previous actions were wrong, and I did not want those wrongs on my conscience. However, at that time I lacked the courage and fortitude to change my actions, thinking that I could play both sides instead. Of course, this did not play out well. Unfortunately, for a time I took the easy route. I kept doing what was expected of my be my homies, whom I knew deep inside really didn't care about me.

> **"There are two roads travelled by humankind; those who seek to live Maat, and those who seek to satisfy their animal passion."**
>
>   - Kemetic Proverb

    'Maat' is righteousness, truth, selflessness, sharing, compassion, and devotion to God, etc. Maat promotes inner peace, social harmony, and contentment. It is equivalent to the Chinese concept of the 'TAO', or 'The Way', of nature.

> **"The wise person who acts with Maat is free from falsehood and disorder."**
>
>   - Kemetic Proverb

    On May 15, 2015, I stopped straddling the fence and committed myself to personal, as well as spiritual, growth. No more gangs, drugs, or alcohol. I made the decision to live my life the way I knew it should be lived. It does not mean that everything became easy and my life was a walk in the park. It increasingly meant, however, that in the face of adversity I could find strength and spiritual inspiration. Now I am able to see the harm that I've caused others, and I'm able to measure my own growth by the adversity I have overcome. I accept, wholeheartedly, that I will have to endure adversity in order for me to live my life in accordance with Maat. I will have to put forth my efforts without seeking reward.

By dedicating myself to personal growth and self-discovery, I have been able to confront my past misdeeds and commit myself to becoming a man of virtue and integrity.

> "The practice of Maat signifies wisdom in action. This is to say that the teachings are to be practiced in ordinary day-to-day situations, and when the deeper implications of this practice are understood, one will be led to purity in action and thought. In order to become one with the Divine, you must become the Divine in thought and deed. This means that you must spiritualize your actions and your thoughts at all times and under all conditions. Actions which present themselves to you in the normal course of the day, as well as those actions which you planned for the future, should be evaluated by your growing intellectual discriminative quality and then performed to your best capacity in a selfless manner. Now action has become a living offering to the Divine. This is the way to spiritualize action so as to move constantly towards the Divine. This is what the East Indian Yoga practitioners call Karma Yoga, or the yoga of action. The performance of action in such a manner that they lead to spiritual enlightenment instead of more entanglement in the world and more spiritual ignorance."
>
> - Excerpt from The-Egyptian Book of The Dead

I have read this excerpt countless times to remind myself that if I want peace and harmony, I have to put forth actions that are aligned with what I seek. Over the past three years I have come to truly understand how Karma works. Being wiser from my past behavior allows me to know, without question, that I cannot get right while doing wrong.

Once I made the transition and began to be my own man (as one might say), I realized that, at the same time, it was not the end to all my problems. However, I had made the leap; and maturity and personal growth followed. Of course, as with all transitions, my own has not been without times of difficulty; for I have made poor decisions. What keeps me on track is knowing that I am not the sum total of past mistakes. Having been able to measure my growth gives me confidence that not only is my future success possible, it is more likely than not. I have a wealth of knowledge of what not to do, that makes the right action that much clearer.

I have learned to be aware of how my actions affect not only myself, but others as well. I've also learned that I have to be understanding and forgiving, because I will need others to do the same for me. I strive to not intentionally bring hardship to anyone else. While I cannot say that no one will be offended by me, I can say that offense will not be caused deliberately.

My story of transformation cannot be complete without the inclusion of those who have motivated, encouraged, and supported me through the bad, and the good, times. My wife of almost nine years (Garolyn Woodard) has been instrumental in my transformation. She saw something in me, and has been everything a wife can be and more. My two children, Adrienne and Adrian Jr., have been understanding and forgiving. We have now built loving and honest relationships that I am grateful for. Although my mother recently passed away, I can not say how much she supported, and encouraged, me to reach my full potential. I can only hope to honor her memory by becoming the man she knew I would become. My sister and confidant, Althena Woodard-Hendricks, has been an inspiration to me and an example of perseverance. In high school she was called "The Brain"; for me, she is my Shero. My childhood friend Koid Starks is the definition of a true friend. Although we may have gotten into some mischief when we were children, as adults Koid serves as an example for me to know what a man is.

I make no excuses for the things that I have done, or the crimes I have committed. Even the things that I never was caught for. I do declare, however, that my transformation is sincere, and I will never commit another crime. It is my believe that, as long as a person is courageous and desires to change, that there is always hope for redemption.

Over the past 25 years that I've been in prison, I have witnessed hopelessness. I myself have been hopeless; the only thing I could focus on being that which was in front of me. There was no room for compassion or empathy to exist, crippling my ability to transform myself. When I first entered prison (1996) there was very little for a person on a maximum security yard to do other than hang out on the yard or dayroom. There were very few self-help groups, or classes. Not to say that men in California's prisons should not be self-motivated to change and grow. In a perfect world that would be the situation. But because our reality is far from perfect, the men that come to prison are more inclined to go with the flow. That flow can be positive, or it can be negative. For a time, I went with that wide negative flow, until I found my ability to catch a positive drift.

In recent years, CDCR has invested in the rehabilitation of the men that are incarcerated, and the results are positive and encouraging. I would hope that CDCR commits more resources towards this positive trend in the years ahead.

Thank you for your time, and any consideration that you might give this writing.

Adrian Woodard
K-03214

BRIAN FIORE

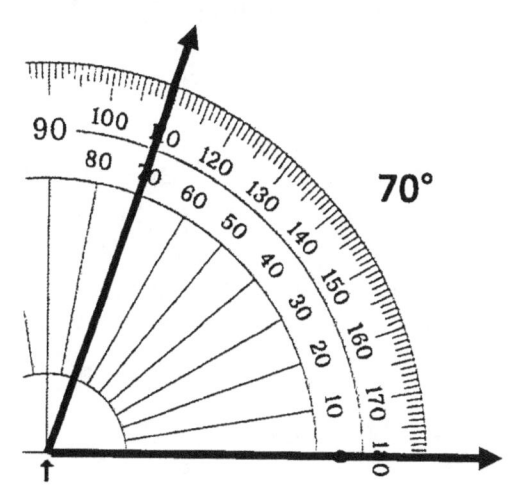

ABANDON COMFORT

The Exponentiality of 1°

In 2017, I graduated from Lake Tahoe Community College, earning a transferable degree in Sociology. At the time I was 27 years-old. Growing up I assumed I would attend college, earning at least a Bachelor's degree in some respected field. However, I did not understand the complexities of life when I was assuming my educational future.

When I finally earned my Sociology degree I was ecstatic. To this very day (I am now 31), it remains the happiest day of my life, and thus far my single greatest accomplishment. It was a day to be celebrated, and I am thankful that my family, and friends, were there to share it with me. The tears, and smiles, on both sides demonstrated how significant the moment was, and just how proud they were of me. Had I stayed on a clear educational path to begin with, It would not have taken me so long to earn my degree. I have learned that when it comes to education, what matter is seeking it out. One should not get hung up on how quickly he (or she) attains education, only that you pursue it.

In my case, I finally sought it out and achieved the first part of my goal toward reaching a Bachelor's degree. Interestingly enough, the graduation did not take place in a typical setting such as a gymnasium or sports stadium. Rather, it took place in a California State Prison visiting room. As happy as I was in receiving my degree I was also extremely nervous. Some might consider it odd that this was not because I was in a room surrounded with murderers, gang members, drug addicts, and those society has deemed too dangerous to be on the streets, but rather because I was to give a speech during the ceremony.

You see, I had come to know these men. They were different from who they once were, and the biggest contributing factor to this change was a chance at receiving an education. Like myself, they too were on an educational journey, striving to accomplish their own goals. My speech, on the other hand, created it's own fear. At the time I was enrolled in a speech class, and I had some experience with public speaking, but I still lacked confidence in myself. In hindsight, I know the anxiety eventually would wash away; I just can not recall when.
Unfortunately, not everything in life washes away as easily as my anxiety did during graduation. I have a lot of regrets in, and wishes for, my life. As I continue to get older, I have come to learn that life is about stages. I have heard some people who refer to them as "chapters in a book". Did I know

that any of my stages would include being a criminal, an addict, a graduate, or a role model? The answer is no.

I am thankful that my path has brought me to a stage of positive change, but I do wish I could wash away my biggest moments of poor decision making. In 2009, I would commit the crimes that in 2012 I would be convicted of first-degree murder, two attempted murders on a peace officer, and other serious felonies. It is because of my life experiences that I am who I am today. I just wish that I could change some of my past. Of course, this is an impossibility. The only thing I can control is my present, and future; and my education will play a critical role in both.

While I was working on my degree through Lake Tahoe's Incarcerated Student Program (ISP), the idea I held about education revolved mainly around institutional based schooling. I now realize that this was too narrow an outlook. Education extends to anything that deals with learning (experiential, peer groups, institutional, etc.), and just as I needed a college education, I also need to avail myself to the self-help education on offer within the California Department of Corrections and Rehabilitation (CDCR).

Self-learning and a school education go hand-in-hand. Thanks to my college coursework, I had finally developed a mindset of change. I was breaking free of warped beliefs by learning to think critically about the world. I started looking towards my future - the next class, the next degree. I wanted to learn as much as I could about communication, social psychology, history, english, etc.; but college alone was not actively helping me to learn about me. My educational future could be bright, but it would only be dim if I did not learn about my biggest educational challenge - myself. Rather than simply looking forward to a future, I knew I had to combine both my new college education with what I was learning about myself through self-help classes to venture into my past. In doing so, I knew I could not only find success in school, but in life itself. It would not be easy, but my future depended on me taking an honest look in the mirror, and finding ways to heal the brokenness within.

I am indebted to all of the men and women who have inspired me throughout my rehabilitation. One of the most important groups for me was the Juvenile Diversion Program. This group helped prepare me to face my childhood fears. We used an analogy in describing our lives up to that point - if two ships set sail at the same time from the same place, but one ship had it's course altered by 1°, after an extended amount of time that seemingly tiny course change would have a drastic impact on it's proximity to the other ship. Not only that; If you wanted to get back to the other ship and share it's course, the effort involved would have to be factored by however long your course was adrift. The more we all examined this analogy, the truer it became for our criminality and addictions. My first crime was not murder, and my first drug was not cocaine. My experiences started small with stealing and a sip of alcohol. This was the start of altering my course by 1°, each progressing act not seeming that much worse than the last. This life course eventually landed me on the rocks because of my lack of attentiveness, and avoiding the warning signs of bad weather. Thanks to the people I have surrounded myself with, I can now track my course back to the beginning so that I can finally travel in safe waters.

I was born in 1989 in San Luis Obispo. Although my family dysfunction was not as bad as some families, it still directly impacted me in ways I would not understand until later in life. There was arguing and fighting in the home between my dad and my biological mom. I remember being told to go outside with my brother (my only sibling, who was 3½ years older than me) as my parents fought, and as I was sitting on the porch I distinctly remember the neighbor staring at me. Coping skills were apparently foreign, but in my young eyes I felt like how my parents handled their issues was the way to do so.

One of the most traumatic things I experienced happened shortly after we moved to the Bay Area in Northern California. I remember that my family was in the car, getting ready to pass the stoplight before the freeway entrance. At the time, we were stopped by a red light and my parents were arguing. My mom handled the situation by opening the door and walking away from the car. I didn't know it at the time, but this would be the last time I ever saw my mom. At five years-old I had no idea of the concepts of abandonment and running away from your problems rather than facing them. That (both literal and metaphoric) car door slamming shut, while nothing was ever said or explained to me about what had happened and why, shattered my internal core.

Eventually, my shattered core would heal, but it would leave a definitive scar, and remain fragile for a very long time. My dad would marry the woman I now call my mom when I was around seven years-old. As I experienced when I was younger, there was still yelling in the house at times. I did not know what a healthy relationship was supposed to look like though, so it seemed normal to me. In my child-like naivete, I was not away of the problems that my parents were having. I know my mom wanted a baby more than anything, but after she became pregnant she soon miscarried. She was devastated, and my dad ended up having a vasectomy without her knowing. With an adult hindsight, I am not surprised that my parents divorced when I was 10. What did surprise me, however, was the moving van I saw parked in front of the house upon my return from school one day.

I did not have a name for the emotions I felt at that time, but I now know them as abandonment, loneliness, sadness, and fear. Whatever had been left of my emotional integrity was packed away onto the moving truck. Once again, nothing about the situation would be explained to me, so my young mind drew the conclusion that I was not good enough; that, just maybe, I was unlovable. Feelings of insecurity would sprout, as well as other character defects due to this family dynamic.

In my eyes as a child, my dad was very authoritarian. Saying like, "I'm not asking you, I'm telling you", were common occurrences, as well as some verbal and physical abuse in the household. My older brother bore the brunt of it, but what I did experience led me to hold fear and resentment, which later turned to anger and hate directed towards my dad, and others, as I got older. Beyond these insecurities, I noticed that my dad would often talk to my brother about his upbringing, yet exclude me. I wondered why, and personalized it, feeling like it was because he must not love me as much. In reality, he did not want to let me know about the trouble he was getting into in case it sent me the wrong message. Where he felt like he was sheltering me by keeping me on the outside of his troubles, the result was that I felt lonely in my own house. Once I became a teenager, my brother started to clue me in on some of my dad's criminal behavior. I was curious about this other lifestyle, and the earlier attempt to shelter me backfired at this point. To my thinking - if my dad did not want to tell me himself, then I would find out on my own.

One of the last dominoes erected that would influence my character defects was the perceived lifestyle that my friends got to live, relative to my own, when I would go over to their house. Most of my friends had video games, nicer clothes, and their parents were more affectionate and easy going than my own. I was envious. I wondered why my home life was not like theirs. I knew we were not poor, so why couldn't I also have the newest thing coming out? I had become extremely materialistic. For some reason, I equated possessions with happiness; but this was false. It was not until coming to prison that

I started to realize the difference between a want, and a need. My dad wasn't refusing to spoil me because he did not love me, but because he knew that I did not need those items. I took for granted the things that I already had in my life, was unappreciated, and lacked the proper gratitude.

As I grew into my early teenage years my home life greatly influenced my psyche. I was not yet cognizant of how everything up to this point had shaped certain beliefs, passed down to me from my parents and other external factors, like friends and media. I was processing information from a broken perspective. At the time I believed that mine was the only way to analyze the world around me. My ability to take a wider view was hamstrung by my issues of abandonment, loneliness, insecurity, and materialism. Adverse childhood experiences such as the way my biological mom literally walked out of my life, my parent's later divorce, and the physical and verbal abuse I suffered left me feeling broken. I did not have any positive coping skills. What was happening in my home life as I grew up would spill into my school, and extracurricular, activities.

My second biggest environmental influence was my school life. Although I enjoyed learning new things, I did not apply myself as I should have. My home life obviously was affecting my behavior. I remember an incident in the second grade when I put my hands around the neck of a female classmate. I did not know how to process my emotions in a safe, and healthy way. Because of what I saw in my home, I believed that this was how I was supposed to resolve a conflict. My school performance was not poor, but it was not excellent either. Most teacher conferences resulted with progress reports marked "N" (for needs improvement) regarding my classroom behavior, and impulsiveness. I cut corners, and cheated at times, as it was easier than actually applying myself.

This was a fairly common theme throughout my education. There would be times I would excel, and times that I fell behind. Some subjects I found more enjoyable, and my grades reflected it. I typically received good marks in math, but I struggled in English. My parents would often stress the importance of school, but I did not understand why. They said that education opens up doors, and would be able to get a better careers, but this was not enough for me. I do not know what would have helped at the time, but I did not take school seriously. The irony is that my mom was a school teacher.

I later learned in my college courses that research done by Carol Dweyck showed how praise can affect learning. Students who received praise for their grades feel good about themselves until they reach coursework that was overly challenging to them. Rather than face disappointment (self-inflicted and by the lack of praise) for an inability to pass a class, students would often cheat and fail to seek help out of a fear of looking stupid. Conversely, students who struggled but received praise for effort not only improved in their coursework, but went on to perform better than students who received praise for results. I realized that I was one of the former students. I was afraid of looking stupid to my teachers and other classmates, so I rarely asked for help. My insecurities flared up during times of struggle, leading to negative self-talk. I was worried that if I asked for help that I would no longer receive praise for what I had been good at, and I craved positive attention. Due to my fear, I fell **behind** at certain points in my education, and it became a self-fulfilling prophecy that further perpetuated the negative self-talk.

School seemed to serve more of a social need than it's main function - education. The people I chose to socialize with continued to influence me. Internal issues that began at home led me to seek out the "cool" crowd. Insecurities and self-esteem issues contributed to my desire to become someone else. I wanted to be a "thug" because (in my mind) they seemed so confident. I could not even fathom the consequences this type of lifestyle, and labelling, would have on my life. Within these social circles school always came second to self-gratification. Even though I was losing track of my life's course, I did not care; I felt accepted.

In high school I became fairly popular on account of my older brother, and my abilities concerning sports. When I was a freshman, my brother was a senior. This allowed me access to his friends, and an older crowd, which made me feel good. Not wanting to be seen as inferior, my pride and fear drove me to behave like them and adopt some of their habits. I believed anti-social behaviors were acceptable because the positive attention it garnered from my peers reinforced my actions.

Despite all of my life's turmoil, the one thing I had throughout my life that was pure was sports. From a very young age I showed signs of having athletic talent. In order to keep his boys busy, and give us an outlet, my dad placed my brother and I in baseball and football leagues. Due to my unique skills I was always one of the better players on the team, allowing me to take on leadership roles, and receive attention. As I grew older I began to play with kids older than me in order to challenge myself on the field. Even though I had always received positive affirmations for my abilities, I was not aware of how good I was until around the age of 10. Since I did not receive much of this kind of attention at home, it felt good to feel needed, and talented. Despite being in a leadership position, I cared more about what people thought of me than I did of others. Naturally, I was liked because I was good, but I was a people pleaser; afraid of conflict. Sports was my ultimate happy place, and I did not want anything to interfere with it.

I believed sports to be my home away from home. I did not have to worry about my parents fighting, I was always needed, people respected me, and it was something I enjoyed. During the games, and even at practice, everything else disappeared for a few hours. All that mattered was the game. I dreamed about making it to the major leagues, or at least the minors. I thought that I would do anything to reach this dream, and because I knew how good I was I simply expected it to happen. My dad told me how hard it would be and that the window of opportunity was slim, but that I had a great chance if I put forth the effort.

Unfortunately, at some point in my life I lost the respect for the game that it demands. I allowed my internal, and external, issues to eventually poison one of the things I loved most - baseball. My dad stressed the importance of taking care of my body, but (as most young people do) I thought I was invincible. Injuries began to pile on, as well as fatigue. During my 11 and 12 year-old baseball season my team played a major league season's worth of games (162). One game, when I got a little older, a teammate's dad gave me Vicoden when I was feeling weak as I was pitching.

This was a quick fix, and it sent me the message that this was an acceptable way to deal with my body rather than listening to it's warning signs when I needed a rest. This was not the last time that I experienced it either. I did not want to let my team down, and I did not know how to say no. I began to accept the false notion that I didn't need any extra work outside of team practice because I had convinced myself that drugs could replace dedication and effort. I believed drugs aided my performance, and when I would do well under the influence this fallacious mindset only became increasingly reinforced.

I used to believe that sports were my main coping mechanism. At an earlier point in my life this may have been true, but once I started to poison my mind with substances, drugs began to fill this role. My life history, and life-style, up to the beginning stages of addiction was dysfunctional. My internal dialogue became dark after my childhood trauma, and I felt broken. I felt like something was missing within me. The missing, and broken, pieces within me all seemed to disappear after smoking marijuana a few times at the age of 13. I truly believed that I had found a special cure to all of my pain. In hindsight, my addiction would blow down whatever dominoes I would set up, good or bad.

    I first smoked marijuana with my older brother, and a friend of his. I did not know what I was getting into in respect to the drug, but the initial emotion for me was a feeling of acceptance. Being included made me feel cool. I did not know the dangers of addiction beyond 'one should not do drugs', but I thought it would not apply to me. At the time, acceptance - versus a concept I did not fully understand - overrode any hesitation. Before starting on the path of addiction, I remember telling my mom that I would never do drugs because my brother had got into trouble over them a few years earlier. I tossed that mindset away quickly, and after using marijuana I felt whole for the first time in my life.

    My drug use started small, and eventually became a full blown addiction. Smoking marijuana went from once a month, to once a week, to every day, and sometimes multiple times per day. My negative self-talk went away when I was high. Life seemed more enjoyable and tolerable, but in reality I was in love with the lies that drugs allowed me. The sweet whisperings I told myself were easier to believe than the truth, and since I was high each day, I allowed the drugs to control the narrative. Drugs seemed harmless enough, and I believed the benefits outweighed the negatives. Since this became my coping mechanism, I never learned how to deal with my emotions in a healthy way. My maturity was stunted because the very period of life I became addicted during was that which learning problem-solving skills is critical to future success. Because I thought that drug use solved my problems, I just stood in my own way.

    As my formative years progressed, my drug use began to include other substances like alcohol, and pills. After a while, I just wanted to feel any kind of high. My drug use became so bad that after a continued period of ecstacy use, I noticed that I was saying my sentences backwards. I stopped using this drug out of fear, but no matter what happened I would never give up marijuana.

    I thought that I was not addicted and could stop whenever I wanted to. I used denial tactics, like comparing myself to meth or heroin addicts, to minimize the severity of my drug choice. My priorities began, and revolved, around getting high. Sports and school always came after. Since my performance did not necessarily suffer in either, no one really suspected just how out of control I was on the inside. At times I contemplated asking for help, but I was too afraid of being revealed as a failure if I did. The drugs were always there to tell me that I did not have to worry about asking for help. They were all the help I needed.

Although I had numerous opportunities to correct my course in life, I failed to take hold of any life preservers. My resentments turned into anger, and my anti-social behavior had taken root from the seeds of childhood dysfunctions. My social environment started to change as my drug use continued, then worsened. Seeking acceptance and being materialistic, combined with a desire to hold a thug-like image, drew me further away from the people I should have sought help from. Instead, I fell in love with the romantacism and glamor associated with the criminal world. I was not satisifed with myself, and this was another way to rebel against my dad, and the world.

I magnified my situation; blaming the world, God, or anyone except for myself. I did not want to take accountability for my choices because it was easier to point the finger elsewhere, and believe that I was not the real problem. I chose to not take school seriously, and to slack off in my sports activities. At every point in my life I had teachers, coaches, friends, and family I could have turned to, but I made the decision to be irresponsible.

I adopted the criminal world as my own, even though (by most appearances) I was leading a crime free life. Even though I tried hard to believe that this was my new label, my true self came through in glimpses; and even in my drugged state I could not seem to run from the truth. I was no thug. I was scared.

Being in such an extremely selfish state, I had lost all remorse and empathy. My criminality moved beyond petty theft to burglaries, drug sales, robberies, and continued on until I committed my heinous crimes. I lacked the ability to care about anyone else because I did not care about myself. My crimes were typically carried out to get money for my addictions, and to prove to my social circle that I was willing to do whatever it took to reach our goals.

As ashamed as I am to admit it, I was one of those criminals delusional enough to believe that I could reach "kingpin" status. This belief became easier to accept as my future, watching movies like "Blow", "Scarface", and

"Paid in Full", and listening to popular rap artists in the Bay Area. The lies I was able to tell myself when I was high furthered the belief in my ability to achieve this goal. My mind only paid attention to quick money and lavish living; it did not focus on the consequences, and suffering this lifestyle inflicted. I wholeheartedly believed that I could escape this fate because 'I would be smarter' than those that fall 'victim' to it. This could not have been further from the truth. Instead of the happy ending I had concocted in my mind, the reality was pure destruction. I terrorized communities, created countless victims, destroyed lives and families, let my friends and family down, and became an embarrassment and burden to society and my family.

It has been almost 12 years since I committed my final crime. During this crime I attempted suicide by placing a .45 caliber pistol under my chin and pulling the trigger. My vehicle then careened off of an embankment on the side of a mountain road, flew out, crashed, and rolled several times. Somehow I was able to climb out of the vehicle, and climb up the cliff to the waiting police officers. I would be convicted of various felonies, totalling up to 68 years-to-life, with an additional three life-sentences.

I am deeply sorry for what I have done. I have no excuses, as there are no excuses. These were my choices, and I will not minimize my actions. Nothing can wash away the pain and suffering I caused to my victims, and their families. I owe it to them, society, and myself to continually work on a living amends, and I thank prison for making this possible.

After coming to prison, I started to realize just how far off course I was. It was in gradual stages, but nevertheless, it was a big change from how my parents had raised me to be. I knew I would be in prison for a very long time. This being the case, I decided early that I did not want to spend it on a main-line yard. I figured that, if I did not listen to my parents who had my best interest in mind, why would I ever want to live on a yard where it would be demanded that I take orders from someone who could care less if I lived or died? This choice was one of the smartest I have made, and it would be the beginning of working my way back to being a better person. I was aware that this change would not happen overnight, but would have to occur in small stages.

My first experience with self-help groups was powerful. I had taken a Basic Alternative to Violence Project (AVP) 20-hour workshop. During the course I was asked what appeared like simple questions about myself, but I could not answer them. After this workshop, I made the conscious decision to pursue learning whether it was self-help programs, education, or vocations. I knew that the more knowledge I acquired, the better equipped I would be throughout my life. After my AVP experience I took a large number of self-help programs. Of all of them, Houses of Healing, Victims Awareness Offenders Program, the Juvenile Diversion Program (JDP), and Denial Management helped me the most on my path to recovery. I was fresh into rehabilitation, and was excited to start, but I was not aware of the work it would require.

In Houses of Healing I learned from the group of men that were in the class. The two things that stuck out the most at the time was the concept of my core-self, and how the other guys shared how the course related to their lives. I started to learn how to apply what a course offered, and how to use the information to start correcting my thoughts, beliefs, and actions.

My experiences with Victims Impact groups helped me learn about empathy. I had to face up to the pain, and damage, I had inflicted on others financially, emotionally, physically, and spiritually. Having stories from victims placed in front of me made me think how my victims must feel, and I felt ashamed of how I had been living my life. I would get stuck in my past actions, but the group helped me realize that, although I need to be accountable, I am also working towards becoming a different person.

When I was selected into the JDP I already had some experience with self-help, but I was not prepared for the deep dive into my past. I thought it was difficult writing my life story in an effort to find my core issues, but when I read my whole story to my fellow mentors and staff, I finally broke down and let it out. This group was instrumental in helping me change; developing into who I am today.

When I took my Denial Management class I had already finished my first college degree, and was working on my second. The class was full of terms associated with avoidance, rationalizing, minimizing, blame, etc. We even looked at some of the techniques used in therapy. The class opened my eyes to the fact that I had lived a life full of denial, and needed to be honest with myself, and others.

Shortly after I took my first AVP course, I was enrolled into Lake Tahoe's Incarcerated Student program, and was part of their first cohort here at High Desert State Prison. I knew that it would be challenging to go back to school, but I wanted to learn. I decided to give school my best effort this time around because my prior attempt were less than satisfying. Most importantly, I would ask for help this time when I needed it. I now knew the importance of raising your hand, and how it demonstrated strength and courage, instead of weakness.

    Education helped me develop stronger writing skills, and improve in subjects I had hated as a kid. I learned to work through problems by analyzing them. The more I learned, the more I started to think for myself; questioning information rather than just accepting it. My college classes started to mesh with my self-help classes, giving me a deeper understanding of emotional intelligence, social psychology, and behavioral psychology. I used everything I was learning to address my current psyche, and my belief patterns when I was younger, to determine the driving forces behind them.

    I finally started feeling a real sense of satisfaction and accomplishment as I completed groups, and classes. Even while I was finishing one, I was looking toward the next. I started creating goals to earn as many Associate's degrees as possible, until I was able to work on my Bachelor's, and then my Master's degrees. I wanted to start creating my own self-help groups, work towards a Drug and Alcohol Counselor Certification, and take specific groups to further my own understanding of myself, and others. When I was younger I simply had dreams. There were no goals because I did not take concrete steps to accomplish anything. I finally have drive, and dedication, to attain what I set out to do.

    My internal problems were being addressed through groups and school, but by working on my internal issues, my external environment changed as well. Prison can be a dysfunctional place, but the space to grow and succeed can be etched out by those willing to put in the work. Some of the men around me wanted to change just as desperately as I did (and do). As we sought the same things, we began to socialize more, and some of us became a tight-knit community; deeply involved in the rehabilitation process. We would go on to earn our degrees, vocations, become mentors, facilitators, and creators of multiple groups. Having a positive social network, rather than the criminal one I used to surround myself with, helped me stay the course towards changing for the better.

    Beyond school and groups, sobriety was the biggest thing I needed in my life. Prison has allowed me the opportunity to detox, and become sober. It took some time, but I was able to clear my mind. I learned that I did not need drugs to improve my life, nor did I need to run from my problems. What

I did need was to learn ways to experience happiness, and cope with negative and positive emotions in a healthy way. I know that I am a recovering addict, and if I do not maintain my sobriety, school and self-help will never work no matter what I accomplish.

Even though my choices cost me my freedom, my new choices have brought me internal freedom. Where I once used drugs as a crutch, and coping mechanism to avoid my problems and emotions, I now use what I have learned (thus far) while in CDCR to squarely face them. With all of the opportunities afforded to me I have no excuse, or willingness, to not take advantage of them. I am proud to say that there are a lot of men in here availing themselves similarly, in an effort to become the best versions of their own selves.

It is a powerful thing to be able to travel within yourself and heal the old hurts; to move beyond the regrets. It is an even more powerful feeling to have hope. After discovering direction in purpose through learning, I now have hope for a bright future. I will continue to work on myself so that I may be productive, no matter where I am. I will make myself of service, sharing my experiences to help others find their own course corrections towards success.

Fiore
AM0057

92

EPILOGUE

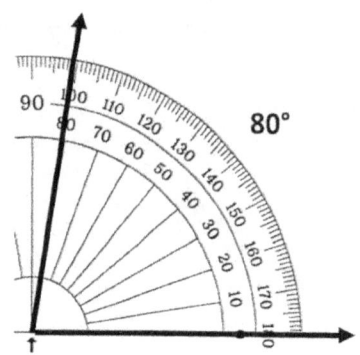

THINK FREEDOM

Hi. I'm Rabbi Brian.

I was mentioned in the forward and in chapter five.

(Isn't that so cool?)

And, now I'm writing the epilogue.

(I rock.)

Assuming you've already read pieces in this book, I have very little to tell you. You've already pieced it together:

> Freedom happens.
> Not just from the outside.
> It's something that happens inside, too.

I am so very proud of the men who have worked so hard, against such hard odds, to liberate themselves.

rB

Rabbi Brian Zachary Mayer

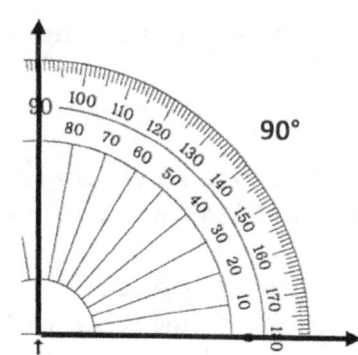

NEXT LEVEL OF THE GAME

END BIG

"The Best Book is the Next Book"

— James Baldwin

Other books by the Authors of "Freedom by Degrees"

- **WRITE OUR WRONGS** (1ST and 2nd editions)
- **EVIDENCE OF LONG, LOST LETTERS**
- **WHY WE MUST INITIATE JUSTICE**
- **PROFILES IN REHABILITATION**

STAY TUNED!

"If You Want to Change, Read a Book. If You Want to Change the World...Write a Book"

— Nelson Mandela